A Guide to

Legal Rights

for

People

with

Disabilities

Marc D. Stolman

Demos

Demos Publications, 386 Park Avenue South, New York, NY 10016

Made in the United States of America.

Library of Congress Cataloging-in-Publication Data

Stolman, Marc D.
    A guide to legal rights for people with disabilities / Marc D.
Stolman
       p.   cm.
    Includes index.
    ISBN 0-939957-59-0 : $19.95
    1. Handicapped—Legal status, laws, etc.—United States—Popular
works. 2. Discrimination against the handicapped—Law and
legislation—United States—Popular works.   I. Title.
KF480.Z9S76   1994
346.7301'3—dc20   94-17955
[347.30613]   CIP

Contents

Chapter 1—*Disability Rights Are Civil Rights*   1

The Creation of Disability Rights Laws   2

What Are the Purposes of the New Laws?   4

Overview of Disability Rights Laws   6

The Structure of the ADA   6

Other Federal Laws   7

State Laws That Outlaw Discrimination   7

The Furor About the ADA   8

The New Laws Require Different Treatment and
New Ways of Thinking   9

Chapter 2—*Who Is Legally Considered
Disabled?*   13

Understanding the Term *Physical or Mental
Impairment* 15

Understanding the Term *Substantially Limits a Major
Life Activity* 17

Working Is a Major Life Activity   18

Other Issues About the Substantially Limits Test   19

Understanding the Term *Record of Having Such an
Impairment* 21

The Meaning of the Term *Regarded As Having*   22

People Who Associate with People Who Have Disabilities   24

Categories Excluded from the ADA's Definition of
Disability   24

Definitions of Disability Under Other Laws   27

Summary   27

Chapter 3—*What About Job Discrimination*   31

What Is a "Reasonable Accommodation?"   32

What Is an "Undue Hardship?"   36

Attempts To Clarify the Definition   39

Who Is a "Qualified Person with a Disability?"   41

The Beginning: Applying for a Job   45

On The Job: Equal Treatment and Equal Benefits   49

How To Establish a Discrimination Case   52

Penalties for Employment Discrimination   55

Summary   56

Chapter 4—*Public Access*   61

What Is a "Public Accommodation?"   62

What Does the "Readily Achievable" Standard Mean?   65

What Is Required of Private Businesses?   66

Alternatives to Barrier Removal   69

What Is Required of Publicly Owned Facilities?   70

What Should You Do If Your Access Rights Are
    Violated?   72

Summary   75

Chapter 5—*Insurance Problems*   77

The Impact of the ADA on Insurance   78

The Right To Be Excluded   79

State Law Protections for People Seeking Insurance   81

Suggestions for People with Insurance Problems   81

Summary   82

Chapter 6—*What Government Benefits are
    Available?*   85

Understanding the Social Security Program   86

Social Security's Definition of the Word *Disabled*   88

Understanding Supplemental Security Income   90

Understanding Medicare   92

Chapter 7—*What Happens If I Die or Become Incapacitated* 97

Wills   99
Trusts   100
Durable Power of Attorney   101
Summary   103

Chapter 8—*What If I Have Problems Paying My Debts?* 105

The Powers of Creditors   106
The Right To File Bankruptcy   108
Preventing Unfair Debt Collection Practices   110
The Right to Accurate Credit Reporting   112

Chapter 9—*How Do I Enforce My Rights?* 117

Making Complaints to Governmental Agencies   118
Hiring a Lawyer   121
Only a Lawyer Can Give Legal Advice   123

Appendix A: California's Statutory Form for a Durable
Power of Attorney for Health Care   125
Appendix B: California's Statutory Will Form   129
Index   139

Preface

This book is about the legal topics most often encountered by people with disabilities. It covers the Americans With Disabilities Act, as well as such issues as Social Security, wills, durable powers of attorney, and other common legal problems. It is primarily written for non-lawyers, but legal professionals may benefit from it as well.

Everyone has legal problems at some point in their lives, and people with disabilities have many of the same problems that everyone else has. However, life can sometimes be more difficult for people with disabilities, and you may have special legal problems that others do not often share.

People with disabilities often encounter discrimination and need to know about the Americans With Disabilities Act (ADA). The ADA protects the jobs of disabled people. It also requires that public facilities (such as restaurants) be made accessible to customers with disabilities if such access can be provided at a reasonable cost. Many readers may have specific questions about the ADA's rules. For those with such questions, I have attempted to provide a comprehensive explanation of it in the first four chapters.

In more than ten years of practicing law in San Francisco, I have heard almost every conceivable legal question. In the second half of this book, I tried to answer the most common questions that readers may have. The laws about insurance, government benefits, wills, trusts, durable powers of attorney, bankruptcy, debt collection, credit reports, and enforcing your rights are explained. Forms for a will and a durable power of attorney are attached in the appendices.

Each chapter lists specific references to the sources cited. This will allow you to look more closely into your specific problems and to stay up-to-date with any changes in the laws mentioned.

I sincerely hope that you will benefit from reading this book and that it helps you with any legal problems you may encounter.

*H*ow To Use This Book

You will find this book easy to use because each of its nine chapters covers a different legal topic. If only one issue concerns you, you only need to read one chapter, not the whole book.

Since the book deals with the legal problems often faced by people with disabilities, the first four chapters review the Americans With Disabilities Act (ADA). The next four chapters discuss problems of insurance, government benefits, estate planning, and debt burdens. The last chapter tells you how to enforce your rights.

The first half of the book explains the laws that protect people with disabilities. If you are interested in the Americans with Disabilities Act or you have suffered discrimination because of your *disability,* you will find the first half of the book most helpful. It discusses the body of American law that is becoming known as "disability rights law."

Chapter 1 discusses the reasoning behind the ADA since it is only possible to completely understand a law if one understands why the law was created.

Chapter 2 explains the complicated legal definition of the word *disability* and will help if you are not sure whether your physical or mental condition is legally considered a disabling condition.

Chapter 3 deals with problems that you might encounter on your job. It explains how employers must help disabled people and discusses job protection from application through termination. If you need to establish an employment discrimination case, it shows you how.

Chapter 4 discusses the ADA's accessibility requirements. All "public accommodations" must make their public areas accessible for disabled people if that is "readily achievable." This chapter defines the terms "public accommodation" and "readily achievable." The new laws are discussed, as well as the tax breaks available to businesses. Finally, this chapter tells you how to establish a case for a violation of the ADA's public accessibility laws.

The last five chapters of the book discuss the most common legal problems that people with disabilities encounter.

Chapter 5 discusses insurance issues, the insurance provisions of the ADA, and the state laws that protect people with disabilities.

Chapter 6 is about government benefits that might be available to you, including Social Security, Medicare, and SSI.

Chapter 7 discusses problems people may have in planning for their own death or disability, including wills, trusts, and powers of attorney. Sample forms for a will and a durable power of attorney for health care are provided as Appendices.

Chapter 8 discusses problems people may encounter if they cannot pay their debts. The laws about bankruptcy, illegal collection practices, and inaccurate credit reports are explained.

The last chapter explains what you need to do to enforce your rights if discrimination occurs. Addresses and telephone numbers of government agencies are provided. The chapter gives suggestions for choosing a lawyer and for making governmental complaints.

You may skip to any part of the book. It is divided into chapters and subchapters so you can skip to the parts of the book that are most important to you at any one time. If you later have another legal problem, you can read the chapter dealing with that topic.

Dedication

To Patou, Andrew, and Elissa

Disability Rights Are Civil Rights

"Historically, society has tended to isolate and segregate individuals with disabilities . . . . —*The Americans With Disabilities Act, Section 12101(a)(2)*

The United States of America was founded with the declaration that "all men are created equal." However, at the time Thomas Jefferson wrote the Declaration of Independence, black people were slaves, women could not vote, and people with disabilities were treated as outcasts.

Since 1776 America has changed its laws

many times in a continuing attempt to guarantee its citizens the equality mentioned in the Declaration of Independence. In 1789 the thirteen colonies ratified the Bill of Rights. In 1863, after the outbreak of civil war, President Lincoln emancipated American slaves. In 1920 women won the right to vote. Until recently, however, people with disabilities were still treated as outcasts without rights to equal opportunities or access to public facilities.

Finally, on July 26, 1990, President George Bush signed into law the Americans With Disabilities Act before a gathering of more than 3,000 people in a ceremony on the South lawn of the White House. He described the Act as a "historic new Civil Rights Act . . . the world's first comprehensive declaration of equality for people with disabilities." Senator Edward M. Kennedy agreed about the importance of the ADA, calling it "an emancipation proclamation" for people with disabilities.[1]

The fact that political leaders of both major parties agreed about the importance of the ADA indicates its significance. The ADA is a curious blend of labor laws, building codes, telecommunications regulations, and other rules. Above all, it is a civil rights act that guarantees equality of employment opportunities and access to public accommodations to people with disabilities.

With the passage of the ADA, discrimination on the basis of disability is now as illegal as discrimination on the basis of race, creed, color, or religion. "Disability rights" are fundamental civil rights guaranteed to all Americans.

These newest of civil rights were created because society needed them and people fought for them. The purpose of the new laws is to assure equality of opportunity and full integration of people with disabilities. National, state, and local laws now protect people with disabilities. The new federal Americans With Disabilities Act requires businesses to take steps to accommodate people with disabilities and even requires new ways of thinking about such people.

T he Creation of Disability Rights Laws

To fully understand disability rights laws, it is necessary to understand why they were created. Most laws are created to fill the needs of society, and the body of American law that is now becoming known as "disability rights law" is no exception. The Americans

With Disabilities Act was not created in a vacuum, nor did it suddenly appear on the landscape of American jurisprudence without rhyme or reason. It had been needed for many years.

The need for disability rights laws came from medical, technological, and social advances. Medical advances have increased the human life span; mishaps and diseases that once were deadly have become in many instances only disabling, and people with disabilities live for increasingly longer periods of time. Technological advances have made even the most seriously disabled people capable of productive employment. Social advances have allowed everyone to realize that people with disabilities are equal citizens who deserve equal opportunities and treatment with dignity. Disability rights laws are simply a legal reflection of these changes in medicine, technology, and society.

The beginnings of disability rights law can be found in the Civil Rights Act of 1964, which defined and expanded the Constitutional guarantees of freedom and equality. It prohibited discrimination against many ethnic minorities in jobs and in access to public facilities. Civil rights activists wanted more than the 1964 laws and saw the plight of Black Americans and other insular minorities as civil rights issues. Martin Luther King, Jr. himself described America's civil rights laws as a "sparse and insufficient collection of statutes. . . barely a naked framework."[2]

In the late 1960s, people with disabilities also began to see their plight as a civil rights issue. Once considered only afflicted objects of pity, people with disabilities began to understand that they, too, had certain "inalienable rights." Civil rights proponents urged people with disabilities to follow the example set by Black Americans in their quest for dignity and equality. One scholar even wrote of "Uncle Tom and Tiny Tim: Some Reflections on the Cripple as Negro."[3]

By the early 1970s, people with disabilities began to insist on their rights to be treated as equal citizens needing equal opportunities and freedom from discrimination. By 1974 disability rights activists used the slogan "You gave us your dimes, now we want our rights." People began to realize that the activists were right; people with disabilities could contribute to America and deserved the chance to do so. Disability rights laws began to be passed. This represented a fundamental change in society's perception of its responsibilities to people with disabilities—from charity to civil rights.[4]

Civil rights activists succeeded in the passage of a growing body of legislation prohibiting discrimination against people with disabilities. The 1968 Architectural Barriers Act required federally funded or leased buildings to be accessible. The 1970 Urban Mass Transportation Act required eligible jurisdictions to provide accessibility plans for mass transportation. The Rehabilitation Act of 1973 outlawed discrimination against people with disabilities by any "program or activity receiving federal financial assistance." The 1975 Education for All Handicapped Children Act provided that each handicapped child was entitled to an education in the least restrictive environment, and the 1975 Fair Housing Act amendments provided for barrier removal in federally supported housing.

These federal laws contributed to a gradual change in the legal position of people with disabilities. In the 1970s and 1980s many individual states also passed laws prohibiting discrimination against people with disabilities. But the state laws were all different, and there was no comprehensive national legal system to protect people with disabilities when Congress began to study the problem in the 1980s. In 1990 the federal government enacted the Americans With Disabilities Act to provide a comprehensive framework of protections for people with disabilities.

W hat Are the Purposes of the New Laws?

"The nation's proper goals regarding individuals with disabilities are to assure equality of opportunity, full participation, independent living, and economic self-sufficiency for such individuals . . . ."
—*The Americans With Disabilities Act, Section 12101(a)(8)*

The goals of disability rights laws are to eliminate discrimination against people with disabilities and to enable them to become productive contributors to society. The new laws require equal job opportunities and equal access to public services, with the goals of integrating people with disabilities into society, which will benefit both people with disabilities and society at large.

In its studies in the late 1980s, Congress found that there were 43 million people in America with disabilities and that the number was increasing as the population grew older. One study presented to Congress showed that two-thirds of all Americans with disabilities between the ages of 16 and 64 were not working at all, even though two-thirds of those not working said that they wanted to work. Many of those polled who wanted to work believed that discrimination was an important reason for their inability to find employment. The poll concluded: "By almost any definition, Americans with disabilities are uniquely underprivileged and disadvantaged. They are much poorer, much less well-educated and have much less social life, have fewer amenities and have a lower level of self-satisfaction than other Americans."[5]

The fact that most people with disabilities were unwillingly unemployed gave Congress a rallying point around which both Republicans and Democrats could agree.

The National Council on Disabilities (NCD), an independent federal agency whose members were appointed by the president and approved by the Senate, recommended that "Congress should enact a comprehensive law requiring equal opportunity for individuals with disabilities, with broad coverage, and setting clear, consistent and enforceable standards prohibiting discrimination on the basis of handicap." Congress followed this recommendation, incorporating some of its language into the ADA.[6]

Congress passed the ADA by overwhelming margins in both the House and Senate. Congress did not mask the fact that employment of people with disabilities was the most important goal of the ADA, since it was meant both to benefit people with disabilities and to decrease dependence on entitlement programs. At the beginning of the ADA, Congress wrote: "The continuing existence of unfair and unnecessary discrimination and prejudice denies people with disabilities the opportunity to compete on an equal basis and to pursue those opportunities for which our free society is justifiably famous, and costs the United States billions of dollars in unnecessary expenses resulting from dependency and non-productivity."[7] These are the goals of the ADA: to make it possible for people with disabilities to find and keep jobs and to make it possible for people with disabilities to be fully integrated into society.

Since the Republican backers of the ADA wanted to end the "dependency and non-productivity" that cost the United States "billions of dollars," employment provisions became the first part of the five-part ADA, called "Title One." The ADA's five "titles" involve employment, access to publicly owned facilities, access to privately owned public facilities, telecommunications access, and the ever popular "miscellaneous."

O verview of Disability Rights Laws

The Americans With Disabilities Act is the comprehensive federal
system of laws protecting people with disabilities. However, many
other state and federal laws also affect people with disabilities. The
interplay between them can be confusing, so it is important to
understand the organization of state and federal disability rights
laws before examining the laws in detail.

Our country has a "federalist" legal system, in which our states
are actually sovereign entities with their own governments but
work together in a federal union. The first rule to remember is that
federal laws are generally supreme and usually overrule conflict-
ing state laws. This is called federal "preemption." The Constitution
gave the federal government the power to pass laws regulating all
interstate commerce, in what is called the "commerce clause." Since
almost every commercial enterprise affects interstate commerce in
one way or another, Congress has the power to pass laws affecting
almost every commercial enterprise in the country.

When Congress passed the ADA, it invoked the "full scope of
coverage of the Commerce Clause of the Constitution." Although
this gave Congress the power to preempt all state laws protecting
people with disabilities, it chose not to do so. Congress chose to
allow all other federal, state, and local laws that provide equal or
greater protections for people with disabilities. Since some federal, state, or local laws provide greater protections, those laws still
exist and are enforceable. Therefore, many matters may be covered
under two or more different laws. You are entitled to rely on and
enforce the law that affords you the most protection.[8]

T he Structure of the ADA

The five "titles" of the ADA are:
1. *Jobs*. This part of the ADA outlaws job discrimination
   against people with disabilities, sets rules for application and
   testing procedures, and provides enforcement mechanisms.
2. *Public Entities*. This title requires accessibility to public
   accommodations operated by public entities. It involves public programs and services, as well as public transportation.

3. *Private Businesses.* This title regulates public accommodations and services operated by private entities. It requires every public facility to take readily achievable steps to make its goods and services available to people with disabilities.
4. *Telecommunications.* This title requires telephone companies to provide services to enable people with hearing and speech impairments to communicate with nondisabled people.
5. *Miscellaneous.* This title deals with several categories, ranging from architectural regulations to transvestites.

O ther Federal Laws

Federal laws that already protected people with disabilities were not preempted by the ADA. The most significant one is the Rehabilitation Act of 1973, which outlaws job discrimination by all federal contractors and recipients of federal aid. The Fair Housing Amendments Act requires barrier removal in federally assisted housing. These and the other federal laws mentioned previously still exist.

In 1990 and 1991 Congress passed other laws to complement and interact with the ADA. In 1990 Congress changed the tax laws contained in the Internal Revenue Code to provide for deductions and tax credits for some business expenses of complying with the ADA. Congress also passed the Television Decoder Circuitry Act of 1990 to require that all television screens of thirteen inches or wider have built in decoder circuitry for displaying closed captions.

The Civil Rights Act of 1991 profoundly impacted the employment provisions of the ADA. It gave people suing for violations of the ADA's employment provisions the right to get monetary damages for job discrimination.

S tate Laws That Outlaw Discrimination

By the time the ADA began to phase into effect on January 1, 1992, approximately forty-five states already provided some forms of protection from discrimination for people with disabilities. For example, California, Florida, Georgia, Illinois, Iowa, Maine, Massachusetts, Michigan, Minnesota, Ohio, Oregon, Pennsylvania, Washington, and Wisconsin were among the many states that provided some sort of job protections.[9]

Many state laws provide far greater penalties than the ADA now offers. For example, California's Civil Rights Act not only forbids discrimination against people with disabilities, but also allows private litigants to be awarded both actual and punitive damages if they can prove discrimination. Since the ADA limits the amount of money that can be awarded to a private party, people with disabilities or their attorneys in states such as California may choose to sue valid discrimination cases under state laws because they may afford them greater monetary recoveries.

You can make this selection of laws because the ADA allows people with disabilities to choose whichever law benefits them most. "A plaintiff (the person suing) may choose to pursue claims under a state law . . . if the alleged violation is protected under the alternative law and the remedies (money amounts) are greater."[10]

This means that there is now a large body of law in the United States becoming known as "disability rights law." It is present at all levels of government, from local municipalities to the federal level. They are still a "sparse and insufficient collection of statutes," as Martin Luther King Jr. wrote in 1967, but are becoming a comprehensive and unified system of protection for people with disabilities.

The state, local, and federal laws all add protections for people with disabilities. Their legal effect is to bolster each other, since people with disabilities are allowed to choose among applicable laws if they need to sue for discrimination.

T he Furor About the ADA

Since so many states already had legal protections for people with disabilities by the time the ADA was passed, it is surprising that a furor arose about the impact of the ADA shortly after its enactment. The ADA passed through Congress by an overwhelming landslide, the House of Representatives voting for passage 377 to 28, and the Senate 91 to 6. However, its popularity had decreased by the time the law began to phase into effect eighteen months later. Many people feared that the financial impact of the law would be devastating. Others complained that the law was vague, and still others dubbed it "the lawyers' full employment act."

One famous columnist wrote an article titled "Regulations To Aid Disabled May Hobble Businesses." The Gannett News Service ran another syndicated article quoting the vice president of the American Federation of Small Business as speculating: "I don't think 800,000 lawyers are going to be enough to handle" the impending ADA. The *Notre Dame Law Review* published an article in 1991 titled "The Duty To Accommodate: Will Title I of the ADA Emancipate Individuals With Disabilities Only To Disable Small Businesses?" *St. John's Law Review* published another article in 1990, "The ADA: Nightmare for Employers and Dream for Lawyers?"[11]

One may speculate that the reason for this furious criticism was simply the advent of something new. Human beings often resist anything new or different, and the ADA was certainly that.

T he New Laws Require Different Treatment and New Ways of Thinking

The ADA added disability rights to the list of civil rights protected by the Civil Rights Act of 1964. It guaranteed equal job opportunities and equal public access, making disability rights fundamental civil rights.

These new civil rights also force individuals and businesses to think differently about people with disabilities. The ADA gives people with disabilities protections that are parallel to existing protections against discrimination on the basis of race, color, national origin, sex, and religion. "However, while the Civil Rights Act of 1964 prohibited any consideration of personal characteristics such as race or national origin, the ADA necessarily takes a different approach."[12]

The "different approach" of the ADA requires employers and public businesses to consider a person's disabilities and to take reasonable steps to accommodate them. One legal scholar claimed that this "different approach" did not amount to "affirmative action," but the technical argument is meaningless. Businesses must now think about people with disabilities differently than they did previously. Employers and public businesses must now think of people with disabilities as potential employees and potential customers. Consideration must be given to integrating such people into the work force and to making them customers.[13]

In the past, businesses may have overlooked applicants with disabilities and ignored disabled consumers. The ADA and the other disability rights laws in our cities, states, and nation require basic changes in society's view of people with disabilities. Once viewed as either pitiable or heroic, people with disabilities now proudly state: "In fact, we are neither. We are just average people trying to do the best we can." Disability rights laws are bringing attention to the ability of so-called "disabled" people to become full participants in American society—as workers, job applicants, and customers.[14]

These new laws have created fundamental new civil rights. They require businesses and individuals to treat people with disabilities differently than ever before and even require them to think in new ways. These changes will have far-reaching consequences that will become increasingly apparent.

R eferences

1. The quote is from President Bush at the South lawn ceremony, Remarks by the President During Ceremony for the Signing of the Americans With Disabilities Act of 1990, 2 (July 26, 1990) (on file with the HARVARD CIVIL RIGHTS-CIVIL LIBERTIES LAW REVIEW). This also appears in Robert L. Burgdorf Jr., *The Americans With Disabilities Act: Analysis and Implications of a Second Generation Civil Rights Statute,* 26 HARV. C.R.-C.L.L. REV. 413, 413–14 (1991). The quote from Senator Kennedy about the "emancipation proclamation" appears at 135 Cong. Rec. S10,789 (daily ed. Sept. 7, 1989) (statement of Sen. Kennedy). *See also* Mr. Burgdorf's article, cited above.
2. The quote from Martin Luther King Jr. appeared in the book by Martin Luther King, Jr., *Where Do We Go From Here: Chaos or Community?* 10 (1967).
3. Leonard Kriegel, "Uncle Tom and Tiny Tim: Some Reflections on the Cripple as a Negro," *38 American Scholar* 412 (1969).
4. The slogan "You gave us your dimes, now we want our rights" is from Terri Schultz, "The Handicapped, A Minority Demanding Its Rights," *New York Times,* Feb. 13, 1977, at E8.
5. The poll presented to Congress was conducted by Louis Harris & Associates. The quote can be found at S. Rep. No. 116, 101st Cong., 1st Sess. 8 (1989).
6. The quotation from the National Council on Disabilities (formerly National Council on the Handicapped) was from the report entitled

"Toward Independence," at 18 (1986).

7. The quotation from the beginning of the ADA about "dependency and non-productivity" appeared at 42 U.S.C.A. §12101(a)(9) (West 1992).

8. The quotation about "the full scope of coverage of the Commerce Clause" is from the Department of Justice Regulations, 26 C.F.R. Pt. 36, app. B § 36.104 (1992).

9. The source for the statement that approximately forty-five states already provided some forms of protection is Sheryl E. Stein, *The Americans With Disabilities Act,* L.A. Law, Sept. 1991, at 32. The source for the examples of specific states providing job protections was Jane M. Draper, Annotation, Accommodation Requirements Under State Legislation Forbidding Job Discrimination On Account Of Handicap, 76 A.L.R. 4th 310, 313 (1990).

10. The quotation about plaintiffs choosing to pursue claims under state law is from 28 C.F.R. Pt. 36, app. B § 36.103 (1992).

11. The famous columnist who wrote the article about regulations hobbling business was Louis Rukeyser, *Regulations to Aid Disabled May Hobble Business,* MARIN IND. J., Mar. 7, 1992, at B7. The Gannett News Service article that quoted the vice president of the American Federation of Small Business was by Allen Cheng and Elizabeth Murray, *Disabled Due Their Place in Business,* MARIN IND. J., Dec. 27, 1991, at B6. The vice president quoted therein was Thomas Latimer. The Notre Dame Law Review article about disabling small businesses was Lisa A. Lavelle, *The Duty to Accomodate: Will Title I of the Americans With Disabilities Act Emancipate Individuals with Disabilities Only to Disable Small Businesses?,* 66 NOTRE DAME L. REV. 1135 (1991). The Saint John's Law Review article was Thomas H. Barnard, *The Americans With Disabilities Act: Nightmare for Employers and Dream for Lawyers?,* 64 ST. JOHN'S L. REV. 229 (1990).

12. The statement about the ADA taking a different approach is from 56 Fed. Reg. 35544, 35545. *See also* 29 C.F.R. app. § 1630 (1992).

13. The legal scholar who argued about the ADA being affirmative action was Jeffrey O. Cooper, *Overcoming Barriers to Employment: The Meaning of Reasonable Accommodation and Undue Hardship in the Americans With Disabilities Act,* 139 U. PA. L. REV. 1423, 1431 (1991).

14. The source for the statement that able-bodied people view people with disabilities in either of two ways, and the quote about just being average people was from Christina Wise-Mohr, "MS, the World and Me: Who Says I'm Disabled?" *Washington Post,* Mar. 1, 1992, at C5. It quoted Patricia A. Wright, executive director of government affairs of the Disability Rights Education and Defense Fund.

two

Who Is Legally Considered Disabled?

"Some 43,000,000 Americans have one or more disabilities, and this number is increasing as the population as a whole is growing older . . . ."
—*The Americans With Disabilities Act, Section 12101(a)(1)*

When anyone uses the word *disabled,* most people think of someone in a wheelchair. However, the legal definition of the word *disability* is much broader. It encompasses 43,000,000 Americans—about one of every six people in the United States, only a small fraction of whom use wheelchairs. This is because the dictionary definition of the word *disability* is very different from the legal definition.

An ordinary dictionary defines the term *disability* as: "1. That which disables. 2. Lack of ability; inability. 3. Legal incapacity or inability to act."[1] These definitions are very different from the legal definition of disability, which varies from state to state and depends on the context in which the word is used. In fact, the definition of the word is so complicated that it takes almost a full page in *Black's Law Dictionary!* The definition of the word *disability* in disability rights laws is complicated and not equivalent to the definition in ordinary dictionaries or to common perceptions. Although the word can legally be used to denote the "want of legal capability to perform an act," the most important definition for our purposes is the definition contained in the Americans With Disabilities Act, the most important law protecting people with disabilities.[2]

Among the 43 million Americans who have one or more of the disabilities described in the ADA are an estimated:

- 22 million hearing impaired people;
- 9.2 million developmentally disabled individuals;
- 2.5 million mentally retarded people;
- 2.1 million speech impaired people;
- 2 million persons with epilepsy;
- 1 million people infected with HIV;
- 120,000 totally blind individuals;
- 60,000 legally blind people;
- 1.2 million partially or completely paralyzed people;
- 1 million people who use wheelchairs.[3]

The ADA's definition of *disability* is divided into three parts:

"(A) a physical or mental impairment that substantially limits one or more of the major life activities of such individual;
(B) a record of such an impairment; or
(C) being regarded as having such an impairment."[4]

An individual must satisfy at least one of these parts in order to be considered as having a disability for the purposes of the ADA.

To fully understand the ADA's application of this important term, one must first understand the fundamental concepts of *physical or mental impairment* and *substantially limits a major life activity*. Then one can understand the terms *regarded as having such an impairment* and *record of having such an impairment*. Finally, when one understands (a) the protections for people who associate with people with disabilities, (b) the excluded categories, and (c) the different definitions in other state and federal laws, one will fully understand the legal meaning of the term *disability*.

U nderstanding the Term *Physical or Mental Impairment*

The first part of the ADA's definition of disability is "a physical or mental impairment that substantially limits one or more of the major life activities" of an individual.

The term *physical or mental impairment* includes (1) any "condition, cosmetic disfigurement, or anatomical loss affecting one or more of the following body systems: neurological, musculoskeletal, special sense organs, respiratory (including speech organs), cardiovascular, reproductive, digestive, genito-urinary, hemic and lymphatic, skin and endocrine; or (2) any mental or psychological disorder, such as mental retardation, organic brain syndrome, emotional or mental illness, and specific learning disabilities."[5]

The term includes both contagious and noncontagious diseases and conditions. It was not possible for the government to list all of the specific diseases, disorders, and conditions that are considered physical or mental impairments, but we know from the regulations issued by the Department of Justice that the list includes:

- orthopedic, visual, speech, and hearing impairments;
- cerebral palsy;
- epilepsy;
- muscular dystrophy;
- multiple sclerosis;
- cancer;
- heart diseases;
- diabetes;
- mental retardation;
- emotional illness;
- specific learning disabilities;

- HIV disease (symptomatic or asymptomatic);
- tuberculosis; and
- drug addiction and alcoholism (with some exclusions).[6]

The existence of a physical or mental impairment is determined without consideration of the use of medicines or devices that may lessen the impact of the impairment. For example, if you have epilepsy, you legally have an impairment even if the symptoms of the disorder are completely controlled by medicine. If you have difficulty hearing, you are considered to have an impairment even if the condition is correctable with the use of a hearing aid.[7]

Since an impairment is a disease or disorder, the term does not include simple physical characteristics, such as eye color, hair color, or left-handedness. It does not include height, weight, or muscle tone that are within the "normal" range and are not the result of a physiologic disorder. Personality traits such as poor judgment, quick temper, or irresponsible behavior are not impairments. Of course, the term does not include environmental or cultural disadvantages such as lack of education, a prison record, or poverty. For example, a person who cannot read due to dyslexia is an individual with a disability, "because dyslexia, which is a learning disability, is an impairment. But a person who cannot read because she dropped out of school is not an individual with a disability, because lack of education is not an impairment."[8]

Some of the other matters that are not considered physical or mental impairments include:

- pregnancy;
- characteristic predisposition to illness;
- homosexuality and some sexual behavior disorders;
- compulsive gambling and some psychological disorders; and
- psychoactive substance use disorders resulting from current illegal use of drugs.
- Obese people may or may not be covered, depending on whether the person's weight is a simple physical characteristic or a recognizable consequence of a physiologic disorder.[9]

These "excluded categories" are examined in more detail later in this chapter.

Some conditions are not in themselves impairments, whereas diseases that result from them are. For example, advanced age is not an impairment, but medical conditions commonly associated with age are. Hearing loss, osteoporosis, and arthritis are impairments.

Stress and depression are two of the most common and troubling problems that may be considered impairments, depending on the situation. For example, if you are suffering from general "stress" because of your job or personal life pressures, you do not legally have an impairment. However, if you are diagnosed by a psychiatrist as having an identifiable stress disorder, you have an impairment. If that impairment is substantial enough to limit a major life activity, it becomes a disability.

Therefore, it is clear that the ADA considers many conditions to be impairments, not just those that require the use of a wheelchair. Hearing problems, speech problems, diabetes, and even some stress disorders can be disabilities.

However, determining whether an impairment exists or not is only the first step in determining if a person can legally be considered disabled. Many impairments are not severe enough to be disabling. An impairment rises to the level of a disability only *if it substantially limits a major life activity.*[10]

Understanding the Term *Substantially Limits a Major Life Activity*

Major life activities are "functions such as caring for oneself, performing manual tasks, walking, seeing, hearing, speaking, breathing, learning, and working." Working is definitely a major life activity, as are sitting, standing, lifting, and reaching. If a major life activity is limited by an impairment, the next question is whether or not the limitation is substantial.[11]

Many impairments are not substantial. People with a minor impairment, such as an infected finger, are not impaired in any major life activity. A man who can walk for ten miles is not substantially limited in walking merely because he begins to experience pain on the eleventh mile, since many people are not able to walk that distance without experiencing some discomfort! On the other hand, some impairments, such as HIV infection, are inherently substantially limiting.[12]

A major life activity is substantially limited if you are:

1. unable to perform a major life activity that the average person in the general population can perform; or
2. significantly restricted as to the condition, manner, or duration under which you can perform a particular major life activity as compared to what the average person in the general population can perform of that same activity.

The following factors determine if an impairment is substantial:

-   the nature and severity of the impairment;
-   the length of time the impairment lasts; and
-   the permanent or long-term residual effects of the impairment.[13]

W orking Is a Major Life Activity

Working is one of the major life activities that may be substantially limited. If you are substantially limited in any other major life activity, your ability to work need not be considered. For example, if you are blind, you are substantially limited in the major life activity of seeing; and there is no need to determine if you are also substantially limited in the major life activity of *working*.

With respect to working, the term *substantially limits* means a significant restriction in performing either a class of jobs or a broad range of jobs. The inability to perform a single particular job is not considered to constitute a substantial limitation.

Note that when the major life activity involved is working, these additional factors can be considered:

-   the geographical area to which you have reasonable access;
-   the job from which you are disqualified because of the impairment and the number and types of jobs within that geographical area from which you are also disqualified because of the impairment.[14]

You would not be considered disabled just because you are unable to perform a specialized job that requires extraordinary skill or talent. For example, a person who can be a copilot but, because of a minor vision problem, cannot be a pilot of a commercial airline would not be greatly limited in the major life activity of working. A professional baseball pitcher who develops a bad elbow and can no longer throw a baseball would not be substantially limited because he would only be prevented from performing a specialized job.[15]

On the other hand, a person does not have to be totally unable to work in order to be considered substantially limited. If you are prevented from performing a broad range of jobs, you are considered disabled. For example, if you have a back condition that prevents your doing heavy labor, you are substantially limited in the major life activity of working because the condition eliminates an entire range of jobs.

O ther Issues About the Substantially Limits Test

Temporary impairments are not usually severe enough to be regarded as disabilities. Broken limbs, sprained joints, concussions, appendicitis, and influenza are not usually considered disabilities, unless they are unusually severe or long-lasting.

If you had a broken leg that healed normally within a few months, you would not be considered disabled under the ADA. However, if your leg took an unusually long time to heal and you could not walk during that period, you would be considered temporarily disabled. If your leg did not heal properly and resulted in permanent impairment that significantly restricted walking, you would be considered disabled.

The availability of auxiliary aids or medicines do not affect the determination of whether or not an impairment is substantial. For example, a person with a severe hearing loss is substantially limited in the major life activity of hearing, even though the loss may be improved with the use of a hearing aid.

Chemically sensitive people sometimes may be considered disabled. It depends on whether or not, given the particular circumstances at issue, the impairment is severe enough to substantially limit one or more major life activity. "Sometimes respiratory or neurological functioning is so severely affected that an individual will satisfy the requirements to be considered disabled under the regulation . . . . In other cases, individuals may be sensitive to environmental elements or to smoke but their sensitivity will not rise to the level needed to constitute disability." For example, if you have a severe allergy to a substance found in most high-rise office buildings, you would be substantially limited in working if you live in an area where many such buildings exist, because you would be unable to perform the broad range of office jobs performed in those buildings.[16]

Other examples of significant impairments include:

- Cerebral palsy that significantly restricts major life activities such as speaking, walking, and performing manual tasks. However, a mild cerebral palsy that only slightly interferes with your ability to speak and has no significant impact on other major life activities would not be significant enough to be considered a disability.
- Severe back injuries. A woman who had been employed as a clerk-typist sustained a back injury that caused considerable pain and permanently restricted her ability to walk, sit, stand, and drive. She was found by a court to have a disability. However, another person who had been employed as a general laborer suffered a back injury but was able to continue an active life and work as a security guard. He was found to be not significantly restricted in any major life activity and, therefore, not an individual with a disability.
- Two or more impairments that significantly limit a major life activity because of their cumulative effect. For example, if you have mild arthritis in your hands and mild osteoporosis that in combination significantly restrict your ability to perform manual tasks, you have a disability.[17]

Therefore, if you have a physical or mental impairment that meets the requirement of substantially limiting a major life activity, you will have met both elements of the first part of the three-pronged test of the ADA. You will be considered legally disabled and entitled to its protection. However, even if you do not meet this first part of the test, you will still be considered disabled (and entitled to the protection of the ADA) if you meet either of the other two parts of the ADA's definition—if you either have a record of a disabling impairment or are regarded as having one.

U nderstanding the Term *Record of Having Such an Impairment*

The second part of the ADA's three-pronged definition of disability protects people who have a record of a disabling impairment. This includes people who may not fit into the first part of the definition because they may not have a present impairment that substantially limits major life activities, but who have a past record of such an impairment.

This part of the definition protects people with a medical or psychological history of a disability, people who have recovered from a disabling impairment, and people who were misdiagnosed or misclassified as having a disability. These people are considered as having a disability whether or not they currently have any impairment that substantially limits major life activities. They are protected by the ADA whether or not the record is accurate.

Examples of people who are considered disabled under this second prong of the definition include:

- persons misclassified as mentally retarded or learning disabled; (People who *are* mentally retarded or learning disabled already fit within the first part of the definition.)
- former cancer patients who have recovered and are no longer substantially impaired;
- people with a past history of mental or emotional illness that is no longer substantially limiting.

If you have a past record of a substantially limiting condition, you are protected from discrimination by the ADA. Employers and public accommodations cannot rely on any such records in making decisions about employment and access. Examples of potential violations of the ADA based on records of impairments include:

- A job applicant was a patient at a state institution and misdiagnosed as psychopathic at a young age. If the person is otherwise qualified for a job and the employer refuses to hire her based on this record, the employer will have violated the ADA.

- A person was hospitalized for cocaine addiction several years ago, but has successfully recovered and no longer uses illegal drugs. If he is otherwise qualified to perform a job and an employer refuses to hire him because of his record, the employer will have broken the law.

These first two prongs of the three-part definition are cumulative; they protect both people with a record of a substantially limiting impairment and people who currently have an impairment that substantially limits major life functions. The third prong of the definition also protects those "regarded as having" an impairment that substantially limits major life functions.[18]

The Meaning of the Term *Regarded As Having*

The third part of the ADA's three-part definition of disability is "being regarded as having such an impairment." This protects people who may not have a severe impairment but suffer from discrimination because others believe they do.[19]

Three basic categories of people fit this part of the definition:

1. people who are treated as if they have a substantially limiting impairment even though they have a lesser impairment that does not substantially limit any major life activity;
2. people whose impairment is only substantially limiting because of the attitudes of others; and
3. people who have no impairment but are treated as if they have a substantially limiting impairment.[20]

If you fit within this part of the definition, you are legally considered disabled and are entitled to protection by the ADA because Congress recognized that society's myths, fears, and stereotypes can be just as disabling as actual physical limitations. In one Supreme Court case, the Court stated that "an impairment might not diminish a person's physical or mental capabilities, but could nevertheless substantially limit that person's ability to work as a result of the negative reactions of others to the impairment."[21]

If you are rejected from a job or denied public access because of the myths, fears, or stereotypes associated with disabilities, you may have suffered illegal discrimination. Congress recognized that common attitudes held by many people create tremendous barriers for people with disabilities. This part of the ADA's definition makes it illegal to deny jobs and public access because of these attitudes.

Some examples of people who are protected by this part of the ADA's definition of disability include:

- People who have a minor impairment that is not substantially limiting, but who are treated by other people as if their impairment were disabling. If you have controlled high blood pressure, which does not substantially limit your work activities, your employer cannot reassign you to a less strenuous job because of an unsubstantiated fear that you may suffer a heart attack.[22]
- People who have an impairment that is substantially limiting only because of the attitudes of others. If a woman has a prominent facial scar, her employer cannot refuse to promote her because of fear that customers or vendors will not want to look at her. People with severe burns often encounter discrimination, and they are protected against it by the ADA.[23]
- A restaurant cannot refuse to serve people because of its fears of negative reactions of other customers to their disabilities or disfigurements; neither can it refuse to serve them because of its belief that an impairment may limit their enjoyment of the goods or services being offered.
- A child with cerebral palsy cannot be excluded from class because the teacher believes that his physical appearance would produce a negative effect on his classmates.
- A woman crippled by arthritis cannot be denied a job because college trustees think that normal students should not see her.[24]
- A person who has no impairment at all, but is perceived by other people as being substantially impaired, is included in this part of the ADA's definition. Even completely erroneous beliefs about disabilities are included. For example, if you are fired because of an erroneous rumor that you are infected with the human immunodeficiency virus (HIV), your rights have been violated. Even if the rumor is totally unfounded, you would be considered an individual with a disability.[25]

Therefore, people who do not have a substantially limiting impairment are considered disabled under the third part of the ADA's definition of disability if they are *regarded* as having such an impairment. This third part of the three-pronged definition of disability protects such people just as much as those defined as disabled under either of the other two parts of the definition. Anyone who fits within any of these three parts of the definition is considered disabled by the ADA, and people who associate with people who have disabilities are also protected.

P eople Who Associate with People Who Have Disabilities

These people are not considered disabled, but discrimination against them because of their association is prohibited. Anyone who suffers discrimination because of association with a disabled person is protected, whether the association is through blood, marriage, adoption, or mere friendship. Relatives, business associates, domestic partners, and caregivers are all protected against discrimination that results from their association with people with disabilities.

For example, an employer cannot fire someone simply because he lives with a person who has AIDS. Similarly, an employer cannot discriminate against an employee because his or her wife uses a wheelchair or has cerebral palsy. Even if the employer thinks the employee's disfigured spouse will not be "presentable" to clients or patrons, such discrimination is prohibited. However, the ADA does exclude certain categories of people from its definition of disability and its protections.[26]

C ategories Excluded from the ADA's Definition of Disability

The ADA specifically excludes several categories of people from its definition of disability and its coverage because of last-minute amendments adopted on the floor of the Senate as it struggled over the wording of the ADA. Several senators attacked the breadth of the coverage proposed for the ADA, arguing vehemently against including pedophilia, schizophrenia, kleptomania, manic depression, significantly low I.Q., psychotic disorders, homosexuality, transvestism, AIDS, HIV infection, drug use, bisexuality, voyeurism, alcoholism, and compulsive gambling. One senator even pointed to a long list of conditions in the *Diagnostic and Statistical Manual of Mental Disorders of the American Psychiatric Association* to show all of the conditions that may be covered by the ADA. Others defended the breadth of the ADA's definition.[27] This debate resulted in compromises that excluded some of the disputed categories from the coverage of the ADA in Section 12211, including:

- homosexuality and bisexuality are not considered impairments;
- transvestism, transsexualism, pedophilia, exhibitionism, voyeurism, gender identity disorders not resulting from physical impairments, and other sexual behavior disorders;
- compulsive gambling, kleptomania, and pyromania; and
- psychoactive substance use disorders resulting from current illegal drug use.

Although discrimination based on a person's current use of illegal drugs is permitted by the ADA, there are still some limited protections for drug users. It is illegal to discriminate against a person who has successfully completed a supervised drug rehabilitation program or who is erroneously regarded as engaging in such use. Addiction is a disability, and an addict is defined as an individual with a disability. However, the protections of the ADA do not extend to current drug use or to actions people may perform because of the intoxicating effects of illegal drugs.

The distinction between "current" and "past" illegal drug use can be difficult since the law does not state exactly how long ago is considered "past" use. One can assume that use of illegal drugs a few hours ago is not considered "past" use. There is no clearly defined time limit, but "current" use is defined as "illegal use of drugs that occurred recently enough to justify a reasonable belief that a person's drug use is current or that continuing use is a real and ongoing problem."[28]

Even current users of illegal drugs are not totally unprotected by the ADA. They cannot be denied health services or services provided in connection with drug rehabilitation based on their current use of illegal drugs if they are otherwise entitled to such services.

For example, a health care facility that specializes in the care of burn victims is not required to treat someone for drug abuse, but it cannot refuse to treat a burn victim because of the victim's illegal use of drugs.

Alcoholism is treated differently than illegal drug use by the ADA. Whereas current users of illegal drugs are not entitled to any protection from the ADA (other than freedom from discrimination in health services or rehabilitation programs), an alcoholic is considered a person with a disability and is entitled to limited protection by the law.

The protections for alcoholics are not absolute. An employer may discharge an alcoholic whose use of alcohol adversely affects his or her job performance to the point where he or she is not "qualified." For example, if an alcoholic is often late for work or unable to perform job duties, the employer can take disciplinary action as long as the alcoholic employee is not disciplined more severely than other employees for the same conduct.[29]

Therefore, the several categories mentioned previously are excluded from the ADA's three-part definition of the word *disability*. People whose impairments fall within excluded categories are not covered by the ADA for those excluded matters, but they are considered people with disabilities if they also have impairments that fall within one of the covered parts of the three-pronged definition. For example, homosexuality is not considered an impairment, and a homosexual is not considered a person with a disability simply because of his or her sexual preference. A gay woman who is also blind is considered a person with the disability of a vision impairment.

The exclusion of these final categories completes the ADA's definition of the word *disability*. Anyone covered under any of the three parts of the definition is considered disabled under the ADA except people in the excluded categories.

The ADA's definition is obviously complicated since it contains these three separate parts. However, completely defining the word *disability* for all legal purposes would be even more complicated since there are so many different laws that define the word.

D efinitions of Disability Under Other Laws

The ADA's definition is only one of the myriad of legal definitions of disability. With different disability rights laws at every level of state, local, and federal government, there are different definitions for almost every one of those laws. Each law may have a different way of defining who is disabled.

Even major states have different ways of defining disability. For example, California state law does not protect mentally or psychologically impaired people from job discrimination. Other state and federal laws also differ from the ADA's definitions.

The ADA's definition of disability was modeled after the definition contained in the federal Rehabilitation Act of 1973. Although this act used the word *handicapped* and applied only to federal contractors or recipients of federal aid, its definition was closely followed in the ADA. Like the ADA, the Rehabilitation Act protected disabled ("handicapped") people from job discrimination. Like the ADA, the Rehabilitation Act also had a three-part definition of disability.

S ummary

The legal use of the word *disability* is much broader than lay perceptions, which may only include a person who uses a wheelchair. The legal application of the word varies from state to state and from law to law. The most important definition is the one contained in the Americans With Disabilities Act, since it is the most comprehensive disability rights law in the country.

The ADA has a three-part definition of disability. The first part of the definition includes all physical or mental impairments severe enough to substantially limit major life activities. The second part includes people with a records of such a disabling impairment; this protects people who have recovered from a disability, people who were once misdiagnosed as having a disability, and others. The third prong of the definition includes people regarded by others as having a substantially limiting impairment, which includes people who do not have a substantially limiting impairment but are treated by others as if they do. Some categories are excluded from the

ADA's coverage; examples include homosexuality, transvestitism, and the current use of drugs.

The three parts of the definition are cumulative. All of the people who are included in any part of the ADA's definition are considered disabled and are entitled to its prohibition against discrimination in jobs and access to public accommodations. These protections can be important; they prevent every public business and large employer from discriminating on the basis of disability.

Therefore, falling within the ADA's definition can be very helpful in many ways, including job situations. Employers must not only avoid discrimination but also make reasonable accommodations for applicants and employees with disabilities. These job protections are examined in the next chapter.

R eferences

1. The quotation from an ordinary dictionary was from *Funk & Wagnalls New Comprehensive Int'l Dictionary of the English Language,* 362, (Encyclopedic ed. 1982).
2. The edition mentioned and quoted was *Black's Law Dictionary* 317 (6th ed. 1991).
3. The source for the breakdown of the numbers of people with different types of disabilities was Lori Sharn, "Accessibility Means a Whole New Life," *USA Today,* Jan. 24, 1992, at 6A (quoting the Office of Special Education and Rehabilitative Services, Centers for Disease Control, as its source).
4. The quotation of the ADA's definition of the word *disability* was from 42 U.S.C.A. § 12102(2) (West 1992).
5. The quotation about the term *physical or mental impairment* meaning any condition, cosmetic disfigurement or anatomical loss, etc. was from 29 C.F.R. § 1630.2(h) (1992).
6. The list of specific diseases can be found at 28 C.F.R. § 36.104 (1992).
7. The examples about impairments being determined without consideration of the use of medicines or assistive devices were from the Implementation Regulations found at 29 C.F.R. app. § 1630.2(g).
8. The source for the statement about impairments not including simple physical characteristics, personality traits, or cultural disadvantages was 28 C.F.R. Pt. 36, app. B § 36.104. *See also* 29 C.F.R. app. § 1630.2(g). The example and quotation about the person with dyslexia and the person who dropped out of school can be found in: Equal Employment Opportunity Commission, Technical Assistance Manual, § 2.1(a)(i) at II-2 to II-3 (1992) [hereinafter EEOC Manual]. This was

also the source for the later statement about stress and depression.

9. The list of matters that are not considered impairments is from three sources: 56 Fed. Reg. 35726, 35727 (1991); 42 U.S.C.A. § 12211 (West 1992); and the article by Chai R. Feldblum, *The Americans With Disabilities Act Definition of Disability,* 7 LAB LAW. 11, 19 (1991).

10. The source for the paragraph about the fact that many impairments are not severe enough to be disabling was 29 C.F.R. app. § 1630.2(j).

11. The definition of major life activities is found at 29 C.F.R. § 1630.2(i).

12. The statements about people walking eleven miles, the inherently substantial impairment of HIV, and the consideration of the major life activity of working can be found at 28 C.F.R. Pt. 36, app. B § 36.104 and 29 C.F.R. app. § 1630.2(j).

13. The factors used to determine if an impairment is substantial are found in 29 C.F.R. § 1630.2(j)(2) (1991).

14. The additional factors to be considered when the major life activity impaired is working is found at 29 C.F.R. § 1630.2(j)(3).

15. The examples of the airline pilot and pitcher were found at 29 C.F.R. app. § 1630.2(j).

16. The statements about temporary impairments usually not constituting disabilities and the statements about chemical sensitivity are from 29 C.F.R. app. § 1630.2(j) and 28 C.F.R. Pt. 36, app. B § 36.104.

17. The example about the broken leg and the list of other examples of substantial impairments that appears at the end of Part B of this chapter is taken from the EEOC Manual, *supra* note 8, § 2.1(a)(iii) at II-4 to II-5.

18. The definition of "record of having such an impairment" can be found at 28 C.F.R. § 36.104 and 29 C.F.R. § 1630.2(k). The source for the examples of the job applicant misdiagnosed as psychopathic and the person hospitalized for cocaine addiction is EEOC Manual, *supra* note 8, § 2.2(b) at II-9.

19. The quotation "being regarded as having such an impairment" appears at 42 U.S.C.A. § 12102(2)(c).

20. The three basic categories of people who fit in the definition of "regarded as having such an impairment" was taken from 29 C.F.R. § 1630.2(l) and 28 C.F.R. § 36.104.

21. The 1987 Supreme Court case quoted was *School Bd. of Nassau County v. Arline,* 480 U.S. 273, 283 (1987).

22. The example about the person with high blood pressure is from 29 C.F.R. app. § 1630.2(l).

23. The examples of the facial scars, burns, and the restaurant are from the EEOC Manual, *supra* note 8, § 2.2(c) at II-10 and 28 C.F.R. Pt. 36, app. B § 36.104.

24. The examples about the child with cerebral palsy and the woman with severe arthritis are from the article by Feldblum, *supra* note 9, at 16.

25. The example about an HIV rumor is from 29 C.F.R. app. § 1630.2(l) and the EEOC Manual, *supra* note 8, § 2.2 at II-11.

26. The treatment of protections for people who associate with people with disabilities, and some of the examples, were found in Feldblum, *supra* note 9, at 25–26.

27. The quote about Winston Churchill and Abraham Lincoln and the entire description of the Senate battle over the excluded categories is from Robert L. Burgdorf Jr., *The Americans With Disabilities Act, Analysis and Implications of A Second Generation Civil Rights Statute,* 26 Harv. C.R.-C.L.L. Rev. 413, 451–52 (1991).

28. The quotation about the definition of "current" use of illegal drugs, the illegality of discriminating against a person who successfully completed a drug program, and the exclusion of such people from health care services is from 28 C.F.R. Pt. 36, app. B § 36.209.

29. The discussion of alcoholism is from the EEOC Manual, *supra* note 8, § 8.4 at VIII-3.

three

What About Job Discrimination?

"No [employer] shall discriminate against a qualified individual with a disability because of the disability of such individual . . . ."
—*The Americans With Disabilities Act, Section 12112(a)*

Title I of the Americans With Disabilities Act outlaws job discrimination and requires employers to make "reasonable" accommodations for employees with disabilities. Title I may be the most important part of the ADA because it will help people with disabilities get jobs and keep them.

Title I applies to every large and medium-sized employer in the country, those having twenty-five or more employees. On July 26, 1994, it will apply to companies with fifteen or more employees. The law does not apply to small employers, defined as those having fewer than fifteen employees.

An employer is legally considered to have twenty-five or more employees if they are "employed for each working day in each of twenty or more calendar weeks in the current or preceding calendar year." The same standard is used to determine whether the employer has fifteen or more employees. Employment agencies, labor unions, and joint labor-management committees are included, but the federal government, native American tribes, and private membership clubs are not.[1]

Many of the crucial parts of Title I are not new. Approximately forty-five states already provided some job protections when the ADA was passed; and the federal Rehabilitation Act of 1973 already protected disabled employees of federal agencies, federal contractors, and recipients of federal aid. In fact, many of the fundamental parts of Title I were copied from the regulations and court decisions that had already interpreted the Rehabilitation Act.[2]

To fully understand the job provisions of the ADA, one must first understand the crucial definitions of:

(A) a "reasonable accommodation";
(B) an "undue hardship"; and
(C) a "qualified person with a disability."

These are the three main concepts of Title I. If you are a "qualified person with a disability," you are entitled to protection by Title I and entitled to a "reasonable accommodation" that does not impose an "undue hardship." After studying this overall scheme of Title I, you can understand:

"(A) the specific protections for disabled applicants in the hiring and training processes;
(B) the specific guarantee of equality in job benefits;
(C) how to document a case of illegal discrimination; and
(D) the penalties for employment discrimination."

What Is a "Reasonable Accommodation?"

Title I requires employers to make "reasonable accommodations to the known physical or mental limitations of an otherwise qualified individual with a disability who is an applicant or employee, unless (the employer) can demonstrate that the accommodation would impose an undue hardship . . . ."[3]

The term *reasonable accommodation* may seem vague and difficult to understand because Congress intentionally left the definition of the term flexible. Critics have clamored for clearer rules, noting that "deliberate vagueness is no less insensitive and invidious under the euphemistic label 'flexibility.'"[4]

Actually, the definition of reasonable accommodation is not complicated. It is any modification or adjustment that an employer can make to enable a person with a disability to perform a job for which he or she is qualified. The accommodation must be effective; if you still could not do the job even with the accommodation, the accommodation obviously is not reasonable. The accommodation must reduce barriers caused by your disability; transferring from a job in Michigan to another company site in Florida simply because you prefer warmer weather does not qualify. Accommodations do not include personal items such as eyeglasses, wheelchairs, or artificial limbs except when they are necessitated by the specific requirements of a job.

The ADA itself defines the term by providing a short list of what *may* be reasonable accommodations. The list includes:

- *Accessible work sites.* This refers to making existing facilities used by employees also usable by individuals with disabilities, including both work areas and nonwork areas such as lunchrooms, break rooms, training rooms, and rest rooms. Examples could include ramping building entrances, rearranging office furniture, or simply putting paper cup dispensers at inaccessible drinking fountains.
- *Job restructuring.* This can include restructuring a job so that its marginal, nonessential functions are performed by other employees. For example, a person who has difficulty writing may be allowed to computerize records, or a mentally retarded person with difficulty remembering the order of performing tasks could be provided with a checklist that can be reviewed at the end of each day.
- *Work schedules.* Part-time or modified work schedules may reasonably accommodate some people with disabilities. For example, if you have a mental disability that requires a midweek psychiatric appointment, you may be permitted to

take a longer lunch break on the day of your appointment
and make up lost time by working late.

- *Reassignment.* Reassignment to a vacant position is an
  accommodation only available for current employees. It
  should be considered only when a reasonable accommodation cannot enable you to perform your current job without imposing an undue hardship.
- *Special equipment.* Acquiring or modifying equipment or
  devices could be a reasonable accommodation. This can
  take many forms; telephone amplifiers and special computer keyboards are only two of the most advanced devices.
  Many effective devices are very simple and inexpensive.
- *Changing policies.* Appropriate adjustments or modifications
  of examinations, training materials, or policies may be
  required. For example, a dyslexic applicant may be given an
  oral test unless reading is essential for the job.
- *Readers or interpreters.* The provision of qualified readers or
  interpreters can be a reasonable accommodation for visually or hearing impaired people; the limitation is one of
  undue hardship for the employer.
- *Other actions.* The last accommodation listed by the ADA
  is the ever present "other similar accommodations for individuals with disabilities."[5]

The Regulations of the Equal Employment Opportunity Commission (EEOC) explain: "There are any number of other specific
accommodations that may be appropriate for specific situations
but are not specifically mentioned in this listing." The EEOC lists
four additional items that may be considered reasonable accommodations:

- *Leave.* Permitting the use of accrued paid leave or unpaid
  leave for necessary treatment;
- *Transportation.* Making employer-provided transportation
  accessible;
- *Parking.* Providing reserved parking spaces; and
- *Assistants.* Providing personal assistants, such as page turn-
  ers for employees without hands or sighted travel guides for
  occasional business trips by a blind or visually handicapped
  employee.

The EEOC regulations list three basic types of accommodations: (1) modifications of the application process that enable qualified disabled applicants to be considered; (2) modifications of the work environment that enable people to perform the essential functions of the job; and (3) adjustments that allow employees with disabilities to enjoy equal benefits.[6]

Telling Your Employer About Your Disability

The regulations envision a somewhat utopian, if impractical, "informal, interactive process," in which the person with a disability discusses the need for accommodation with his or her employer. Since the employer's duty to make changes does not begin until he or she knows about the disability, it is probably advisable to tell your employer if you believe that your disability requires accommodation. The EEOC says that the employer and employee should "identify the precise limitations imposed by the disability and explore potential accommodations that would overcome those limitations."

The EEOC envisions a four-step process of identifying reasonable accommodations: 1) after notifying your employer of the need for accommodation, you and your employer are to review your particular job to determine its purpose and essential functions; 2) discuss your specific limitations and identify the problems caused by it; 3) discuss potential accommodations; and 4) select an accommodation, if there is one, that does not impose an undue hardship. The employer is free to choose among effective accommodations and may choose the least expensive one as long as it works.[7]

These new laws attempt to "level the playing field" for employees with disabilities by requiring that employers make reasonable changes to help employees overcome the functional limitations imposed by their disabilities. You are not relieved of your duty to do your job well, and employers are not required to hire a less qualified or less competent person simply because that person has a disability.

Here are some examples of reasonable accommodations:

- Permitting an employee to provide his or her own accommodation. If you are blind, it would be reasonable for your employer to permit you to use your guide dog at work.[8]

- If the employee lunchroom is inaccessibly located on an upper floor with no elevator, your employer may be required to provide a portable ramp or a room on the first floor. The facility does not have to be exactly the same as the room on the upper floor, but it should provide food, beverages, and space for coworkers to dine with you.

- Employers are not required to provide personal items such as eyeglasses, wheelchairs, or prosthetic limbs. However, if your office has deep pile carpeting that makes it impossible to use a wheelchair, your employer may need to replace the carpet or place a usable surface over it.[9]

- You are not legally entitled to have a second person hired to perform any essential duties of the job you seek. For example, if you are legally blind and seek a job as a security guard who reads employee identification cards, you cannot require the employer to hire a second employee to read the cards for you. The limitation on the need to make such an accommodation is the employer's "undue hardship."[10]

There are endless examples of things that could constitute reasonable accommodations because of the endless varieties of disabilities and different job situations. In essence, a "reasonable accommodation" is any modification or adjustment to a job, an employment practice, or the work environment that makes it possible for people with disabilities to obtain and perform jobs. The definition of "reasonable accommodation" is extremely broad.

The requirement to make modifications is not absolute. When Congress shifted the burden of employing people with disabilities to private employers, it limited the amount of money they must spend. Employers need not incur an "undue hardship" in providing accommodations.

W hat Is an "Undue Hardship?"

Although employers must provide reasonable accommodations for employees with disabilities, they are not required to take steps that would cause their own bankruptcy or fundamentally change their business. Employers can be required to spend significant sums to accommodate people with disabilities, but they need not take any action that would impose an "undue hardship."

By limiting the employer's obligations in this way, Congress has attempted to balance society's need to employ people with disabilities against individual employers' needs to run efficient and cost-effective businesses, and to protect employers from endless litigation, unrealistic demands, and overwhelming costs. Justice Thurgood Marshall, writing a unanimous court decision about the Rehabilitation Act, discussed the need to "be responsive to two powerful but countervailing considerations." The definition of undue hardship tries to balance these two opposing concerns.[11]

The definition of "undue hardship" is controversial because the standard is vague. Congress's solution of letting the matter be decided by the courts has left employers cold and uncomfortable at best.

The ADA defines undue hardship as "an action requiring significant difficulty or expense," when considered in light of:

"(i) the nature and cost of the accommodation needed . . .
(ii) the overall financial resources of the facility or facilities involved . . . the number of persons employed . . . the effect on expenses and resources, or the impact on . . . operation of the facility;
(iii) the overall financial resources of the covered entity; the overall size of the business . . . and
(iv) the type of operation . . . the fiscal relationship of the facility or facilities in question to the covered entity."[12]

The EEOC regulations explain that this "takes into account the *financial realities of the particular employer* . . . but is not limited to financial difficulty. 'Undue hardship' refers to any accommodation that would be unduly costly, extensive, substantial, or disruptive, or that would fundamentally alter the nature or operation of the business."[13]

The size and financial resources of the employer are, therefore, the critical components in deciding if a proposed job change is an undue hardship. Large businesses must spend more than small ones because they can afford to. Small businesses are not required to make accommodations that may be required of larger ones. No business is required to change the fundamental nature of its operation.

For example, an independently owned fast-food franchise may appear to be part of a larger entity with national advertising and a huge budget. However, if its only relationship with the national organization is the payment of a franchise fee, only the financial resources of the independent franchisee must be considered.

Only the net cost of the accommodation is considered. Employers may be eligible for tax credits and deductions for providing accommodations. Other sources of financing may also apply. State vocational grants and even charitable donations are sometimes available, or an employee may absorb that portion of the cost that would make the accommodation unduly expensive. For example, if an assistive device costs $2,000 and an employer can demonstrate that his spending more than $1,500 would cause an undue hardship, he should offer the employee the option of contributing the additional $500.

Cost is not the only factor considered in determining undue hardship. Businesses are not obligated to alter the *type* of operation they provide. If a visually impaired woman applied for a waitress job at a dimly lit nightclub, she could not compel the employer to use bright lighting that would destroy the ambience of the club so that she could see! If another employee requested that a thermostat be raised to accommodate his disability, but doing so would make it uncomfortably hot for other employees or customers, this accommodation would also be an undue hardship (but the employer should consider providing a small space heater).

Other examples of accommodations that may or may not constitute undue hardships include:

- Making a temporary construction site accessible to employees who use wheelchairs would probably be an undue hardship, as it might fundamentally alter the nature of the site or be unduly costly.
- Reassignment to vacant positions may violate the terms of collective bargaining agreements. If a worker with a bad back requests reassignment to a clerical job because he can no longer do heavy labor, his reassignment may violate a union agreement with specific seniority lists. Both the union and the employer are required by the ADA to provide reasonable accommodations, but a judge can consider the terms of such collective bargaining agreements in deciding if the reassignment is an undue hardship.

- Negative impact on the morale of other employees caused by accommodations do *not* constitute an undue hardship. Restructuring a job to accommodate your disability by creating heavier workloads for your coworkers may be considered an undue hardship. However, complaints on the part of other employees because you are allowed a "special privilege" of an unpaid leave or a flexible schedule is *not* undue hardship.
- The need for kidney dialysis treatment that is only available on two weekdays could cause an undue hardship on your employer, depending on the nature of your work and whether you could do it on weekends instead of the usual weekdays.[14]

From these examples, one can see that the definition of undue hardship is tailored to the individual situation of each employer. Since the idea is to avoid unduly hurting businesses, "undue hardship" depends on the facts of each case, including the employer's finances. This means that the specific application of the undue hardship defense will be decided on a case-by-case basis.

A ttempts To Clarify the Definition

Many commentators and industry groups wanted clearer definitions so that employers would know exactly what their obligations were. One senator even called the proposed ADA "a legislative Rorschach test, an inkblot whose meaning and significance will be determined through years of costly litigation."

One cannot blame employers for wanting clearly defined rules—even onerous ones—so that they at least know what is required! Employers complain that the vagueness of the undue hardship standard makes litigation inevitable. They even claim: "The outlook is bleak. There will likely be a deep resentment of the disabilities rights movement stemming from 'perverse' results under the ADA." They predict a "backwash of bitterness."[15]

Congress rejected clearly set standards for a number of reasons. The House Judiciary Committee rejected a proposal that would have maximized the costs of required accommodations at 10 percent of a disabled employee's salary because this would have worked against lower income employees. Instead, Congress kept the "flexible" standard; it has already been interpreted dozens of times in court cases stemming from the Rehabilitation Act of 1973. Although this standard requires one to study the facts of each case in light of the four issues that comprise undue hardship, the standard has been working for almost two decades with respect to federal agencies, contractors, and recipients of federal aid.

Some state laws set clearly defined limits. In Massachusetts the maximum required accommodation is $50 per handicapped person, whereas in Virginia it is $500. North Carolina's system has a cap of 5 percent of an employee's salary or annualized hourly wage. Congress rejected these formulas after much debate, preferring the much broader requirement that is now in the ADA.

One of the reasons for this more aggressive approach is that most accommodations are not very expensive. The Senate Committee on Labor and Human Resources estimated that, of all workers who will need accommodations, 15 percent will require no expense at all, and another 15 percent will require a one-time expense of less than $100. A 1982 U.S. Department of Labor study found that 81 percent of accommodations cost less than $500.[16]

Since the majority of accommodations required under Title I are inexpensive, Congress chose the flexible, albeit difficult to apply, standard now found in Title I. Critics still claim it is so vague it is "no standard at all." They correctly point out that "even judges who are given the exact same facts cannot agree on the reasonableness of proposed accommodations . . . . If those who are learned in the law and are enjoying relatively limitless access to legal research cannot agree on whether a given accommodation would be a reasonable one or an undue hardship, how is a small business owner to know what he or she is supposed to do?"[17]

How To Apply the Undue Hardship Standard

In spite of the vagueness of the reasonable accommodation and undue hardship standards, you can apply the four parts of the ADA's test of undue hardship without being a lawyer or a judge. Keep in mind the nature and cost of the accommodation you need, the size of the company or business that employs you, its financial resources, and the type of operation involved. Your view of the situation can be just as insightful as that of a lawyer, particularly if you try to use common sense and keep in mind the employer's viewpoint. Five hundred dollars may not sound like much to you, but it may seem substantial to a small employer!

Being reasonable in your requests may go a long way toward getting and keeping the job you desire. Employers need good workers, and part of the ADA's mission is to expand the labor force by bringing people with disabilities into it. Employers seek an employee who will do a job and do it well; they may be quite willing to go the extra mile for you, particularly if you are qualified to perform the essential functions of the job. What you should strive to be is not a quarrelsome applicant, but a "qualified person with a disability."

W ho Is a "Qualified Person With a Disability?"

Understanding this phrase is crucially important to understanding the employment parts of the ADA, because employers are not required to hire a person with a disability *just because* he or she is disabled. Employers can hire the most qualified applicant they can find and can refuse to hire an applicant with a disability if another applicant is more qualified. Employers need not lower their qualification standards or hire unproductive workers.

- For example, if an employer requires typists to accurately type seventy-five words per minute, he or she need not accept applicants who type only sixty-five words per minute. If a hotel requires its maids to clean sixteen rooms per day, it need not accept an applicant who can clean only ten rooms.

Employers are not required to explain *why* they insist on such standards. Employers need not hire a disabled applicant who does not qualify for a job or cannot perform its essential functions. They can insist that a disabled employee be "a qualified individual with a disability."

The ADA defines a qualified individual with a disability as "an individual with a disability who, with or without reasonable accommodation, can perform the essential functions of the employment position that such individual holds or desires."

Determining if you meet this definition involves a two-step process. First, you must possess the qualifications for the job; you must "satisfy the requisite skill, experience, education and other job-related requirements" of the position. This includes possessing the appropriate educational background, credentials, and licenses.[18]

- For example, the first step in determining if a paraplegic applicant is qualified for a position as a certified public accountant is to examine her credentials to determine that she is in fact a CPA. Similarly, if a law firm hires only lawyers who have graduated from accredited law schools and passed the bar examination, an applicant would not be qualified unless he or she had done so.[19]

Second, you must be able to perform the essential functions of the job. "The purpose of this second step is to ensure that individuals with disabilities who can perform the essential functions of the positions . . . are not denied employment opportunities because they are not able to perform marginal functions of the position." The decision of which functions of a job are essential can be critical, since you may be able to perform some, but not all, job duties.[20]

The "essential functions" are those functions that the employee must be able to perform either unaided or with a reasonable accommodation. They are the "fundamental job duties." However, the process of determining which functions of a job are really "essential" can be difficult, since some employers may argue that all job duties are essential, while people with disabilities may be able to perform only some of them. The determination involves examining the job to decide which functions are essential and which are marginal.

The EEOC regulations say that a job function could be essential for many reasons but list three possibilities:

1. A job duty may be essential because the position exists to perform that function. For example, if you are hired to proofread documents, the ability to proofread accurately is an essential function, since it is the very reason for your job's existence! For a company that needs a "floating"

supervisor to substitute when regular supervisors on day, night, or graveyard shifts are absent, the ability to work any time of day is essential.

2. A function may be essential because there may be a limited number of other employees available to perform the function. For example, a company may have periods of very heavy activity alternating with less active periods. The heavy work flow during the busy periods may make performance of each part of a job essential during those periods.

3. A function may be essential because it is highly specialized. For example, a company that wishes to expand its business with Japan may find it essential that its new sales representative speak fluent Japanese.[21]

Determining which job functions are essential can cause disagreements, as is shown by the many lawsuits involving the Rehabilitation Act of 1973. Employers cannot refuse an applicant with a disability merely because he or she is unable to perform some marginal duties that are not essential to a job, and to many employers this seems unreasonable. If one applicant can run errands on occasion but a blind applicant cannot drive, why should the employer hire the blind person? Because the blind applicant may be able to perform all of the other duties of the job, and occasional errands may not be essential.

Examples of essential and nonessential job duties include:

- An employer may state that a file clerk must answer the telephone, but if the job duties really only entail filing and retrieving materials, and the phones can easily be answered by others, answering the telephone would not be essential. If you have a hearing impairment that interferes with your use of the telephone, you would still be able to perform the job's essential functions and could not be fired because of your difficulty with the telephone.

- In another office, it may be essential for a file clerk to occasionally answer the phone. For example, if there are only a few employees in a busy office and each has to perform other tasks, it may be "essential" for each to be able to use the telephone.

- Some functions of a job may be so important that they are essential even if they are seldom, if ever, needed. For example, a firefighter may seldom, if ever, need to carry an unconscious person from a burning building, but this function is so important when it is needed that it is considered essential.
- A job description may state that typing is a function of a receptionist's job. However, if the employer has seldom or never required the receptionist to type, this would not be considered an essential job function.[22]

Evidence of Essential Functions

The EEOC regulations include seven types of things that can be used to show that a function is essential. In any court debate, the parties can use, among other evidence:

1. The employer's judgment of which functions are essential is the first item of evidence listed in the EEOC regulations, but it is only one factor to be considered. The employer can insist on standards such as typing seventy-five words per minute, but must apply the standard evenly, not use it as a subterfuge to eliminate people with disabilities.
2. A written job description prepared before advertising or holding job interviews is usually very good evidence of essential job duties. However, job descriptions are only one factor to be considered as evidence, as they sometimes are not accurate. For example, an old job description may state that a person must manually read temperature or pressure gauges that are now automatically controlled by computer. A description may state that a dockworker must pick up and carry heavy sacks, whereas all that is really needed is moving the sacks, and the use of a dolly would allow a person with a disability to perform the job.
3. The amount of time spent performing the function is more evidence to help determine if a duty is essential. For example, if you spend most of your time operating one machine, one would presume that operating it is essential to doing your job.
4. The consequences of not requiring the employee to perform the function can be important. For example, an airline

pilot spends very little time landing an airplane, but landing is definitely an essential function of any pilot's job!

5. The terms of collective bargaining agreements often list the essential duties of jobs, but this also is only one piece of evidence in court and could be proven wrong.

6. The work experience of individuals who formerly held the job is evidence of the job's essential duties. For example, if a file clerk had never been required to run an errand, this would be evidence that running errands is not essential.

7. The work experience of other people holding similar jobs is more evidence of a job's essential functions. For example, computer operators may find that it is not necessary to visually read information on a screen, since adaptive devices and braille keyboards can make reading unnecessary.[23]

Summary of the Three Main Concepts of Title I

If you have the required qualifications for a job and can perform its essential functions, your employer must consider you equally with applicants who do not have disabilities. If a reasonable change in the job or workplace can permit you to perform the job's essential duties, your employer must make that change, as long as the nature or cost of the change does not cause an undue hardship.

Only "qualified individuals with disabilities" are protected by Title I. It does not apply to people who cannot perform the essential functions of a job even with the "reasonable accommodation." However, when Title I does apply, it covers the entire job process, including the application itself. It applies from the beginning of the application process through job training, to promotions and distribution of benefits.

The Beginning: Applying for a Job

The ADA outlaws discrimination in job recruitment, application, and interviewing. In fact, Section 12112 alone contains over one and one-half pages of specific rules about preemployment inquiries, entrance examinations, qualification standards, and application procedures! The procedures must be fair, nondiscriminatory, and must provide equal opportunities for people with disabilities.

The employer's obligations begin when he or she seeks job applicants and interviews them. ADA Section 12112 outlaws discrimination in job application procedures, discrimination affecting "opportunities," and even the use of standards that "have the effect of discrimination on the basis of disability." Employers are required to administer tests and applications in a fair and equal manner. Any advertisements reading "disabled need not apply" are obviously illegal; Title I goes far beyond that.

First, the employer must make the interview and application site accessible, as long as doing so does not impose an undue hardship. Applicants with disabilities must be accommodated to enable them to fill out the initial applications and take any required tests.

- For example, a dyslexic applicant should be given the opportunity to take an oral test unless the essential functions of the job require reading. A deaf applicant should be allowed a written test rather than an oral one.[24]
- If an advertisement provides only a telephone number to call for information, a TDD (Telecommunication Device for the Deaf) or relay service should be provided unless it would impose an undue hardship. (Title IV of the ADA requires all telephone companies to establish relay services for deaf people by July 1993.)[25]

After you have arrived for the application or interview, the employer cannot ask if you have a disability. Application forms cannot ask about disabilities or contain lists of impairments with boxes to check in the affirmative or negative. It is even illegal to ask questions such as "Have you had any major illnesses in the past five years?" If you have an obvious disability, you cannot be asked about its severity, nature, prognosis, or the condition causing it. Instead, employers are limited to asking about your ability to perform job-related functions. Employers can ask "How will you do the job?" or "Can you demonstrate how you will do the job?"

- For example, if you have one leg and are applying for a job as a home washing machine repairman, the employer can ask you how you intend to climb stairs to repair washing machines, but he cannot ask how you lost the leg or if you have another impairment.

- If you are asked to demonstrate how you are able to do the job, you must either be given the aid you need to do the job or be allowed to explain how you plan to do the job with such aid.

- If you have an obvious disability that does not affect job performance, you cannot be asked to perform a demonstration unless all other applicants in the same category are also asked to do so.

- One exception is for federal contractors covered under Section 503 of the Rehabilitation Act. They can invite applicants to identify themselves as people with disabilities, since they are already required to provide affirmative action. A few other programs, such as Labor Department programs for veterans with disabilities, also allow inquiries.[26]

Medical Examinations

An employer cannot require you to take a preemployment medical test unless you have already been given a conditional offer of employment, and (a) all entering employees of the same class are subjected to the same examination, regardless of disability; and (b) the results of the examination are kept confidential and used only for informing supervisors of necessary restrictions and accommodations, or for informing safety personnel or government agencies as required.

If the medical test reveals a disability, it can only be used to screen people with disabilities for reasons that are job-related and consistent with business necessity and to determine that they cannot perform essential job functions even with reasonable accommodation. Even uniformly applied medical standards (which have a greater impact on people with disabilities) are illegal unless they meet these requirements. If the employer declines to hire you because of a risk to your health or the health of others, the risk cannot be speculative or remote; it must be a significant risk of substantial harm based on the most current medical knowledge available.

- For example, a firm cannot refuse to hire you because it discovers a disability that is not covered by the company insurance plan, such as diabetes, or because the costs of medical or workers compensation insurance would increase.
- If a medical examination reveals that you have epilepsy and are seizure-free or have adequate seizure warning, it would be illegal to disqualify you from a job operating a machine because of fear that you may hurt yourself or others. However, if the examination reveals seizures that result in loss of consciousness and there is evidence of a significant risk of substantial harm, you may legally be denied the job.
- Tests for illegal drugs are not considered medical examinations and are not prohibited by the ADA. They may be given at any time as long as their use does not violate any other laws.[27]

An employer may use any other kind of test necessary to determine if you are qualified for the job. However, if tests tend to screen out people with disabilities, the employer must prove that the test is job-related and consistent with business necessity. Even if the test is job-related and justified by business necessity, applicants with disabilities must be given reasonable accommodations to enable them to score fairly if the employer knows about the disability. This is to ensure that the tests "accurately reflect a person's job skills, aptitudes, or whatever else the test is supposed to measure, rather than the person's impaired skills."[28]

An employer cannot refuse to hire you because of the cost of making a reasonable accommodation that does not impose an undue hardship. ADA Section 12112(b)(5)(B) specifically prohibits denying a job application "based on the need of the covered entity to make reasonable accommodation to the physical or mental impairments of the employee or applicant."

The entire process of applying for jobs is required to be fair and administered without discrimination. Applicants are entitled to reasonable accommodations from the very beginning, and they cannot be asked many of the questions that employers have asked in the past. The ADA's ban on discrimination does not end when you are hired to perform a job. The protections of Title I continue through the entire employment process, guaranteeing equal benefits, opportunities for advancement, and compensation.

O n the Job: Equal Treatment and Equal Benefits.

Section 12112 of the ADA prohibits discrimination on the basis of disability in job "advancement, or discharge of employees, employee compensation, job training, and other terms, conditions, and privileges of employment." In other words, its protections apply as long as you work at the job.

Of course, you are entitled to reasonable accommodations that do not impose undue hardships on your employer. These can include an accessible work site, a flexible schedule, and any of the other matters discussed previously. You are also entitled to all of the benefits of the job; your disability cannot cause you to be limited, segregated, or classified in a way that adversely affects your opportunities.

The EEOC Regulations state you must have equality with other employees in:

- upgrading, promotion, award of tenure, demotion, transfer, layoff, termination, right of return from layoff, and rehiring;
- rates of pay or any other form of compensation;
- assignments, classifications, organizational structures, position descriptions, lines of progression, and seniority lists;
- leaves of absence, sick leave, or other leave;
- fringe benefits;
- selection and financial support for training, including apprenticeships, meetings, conferences, and leaves of absence for training;
- activities sponsored by the employer, including social and recreational programs; and
- any other term, condition, or privilege of employment.

Job Advancement and Discipline

Employers cannot discriminate in job evaluations, advancement, training for advancement, discipline, and discharge. Some employers may assume that you are not interested in or qualified for advancement because of your disability; this is patently illegal. The employer cannot refuse to promote you because of the need to make a reasonable accommodation unless it would impose an undue hardship. Even "separate but equal" treatment is not allowed; you cannot be placed in separate lines of progression or in segregated units because of your disability.

This means that you must have an equal chance to participate in training programs that lead to advancement, and reasonable accommodations must be provided to make such programs accessible and available. Materials should be provided in accessible formats for people with visual problems, hearing impairments, or learning disabilities. Interpreters and notetakers may even be required if no undue hardship is imposed.

An employer cannot avoid its responsibility to give you accommodations in training programs by hiring an outside company to do the training. That outside company's facilities should be made accessible, and the other provisions of Title I must be followed. Company conferences held in hotels should also be accessible; the employer remains responsible for the conference or training course.

In job performance, a person with a disability must do his job as well as every other employee. His employer can hold him to the same standards of production and performance as his coworkers; the employee cannot use his disability as an excuse for not working. The disability only comes into play if it *causes* low performance, in which case the employer is required to provide a reasonable accommodation that does not impose any undue hardship.

An employer need not evaluate a person with a disability on a lower standard or discipline him less severely than his coworkers. He is entitled to *equal* job opportunities and to reasonable accommodations for his disability. If he performs poorly and his poor work is not related to his disability, his employer can discipline him just as he can discipline every other employee in the company. He is not a "qualified individual with a disability" if poor performance is the result of his disability and no reasonable accommodation exists (without undue hardship) that will enable him to perform the essential job functions. His employer can reassign or terminate him after exploring the possibilities for accommodation.

Discrimination in compensation is also illegal. You are entitled to equal pay. Your pay cannot be reduced because of your disability, not even because of your inability to perform marginal duties that are not essential job functions. However, if you are reassigned to a part-time job, you are not entitled to full-time pay.[29]

All compensation must be equal, including full benefits. This includes insurance; you must be given equal access to whatever plan the employer provides. However, if the company plan excludes preexisting conditions, you are not entitled to insist on other insurance. Employers' plans are allowed to contain clauses limiting coverage of preexisting conditions, and the plan can limit yearly coverage for certain types of procedures or treatments as long as they are uniformly applied to all employees, not just to those who have a disability.[30]

If your firm offers medical examinations to its employees, it cannot make you take the exam unless it is job-related and consistent with business necessity. This is basically the same legal requirement for medical examinations given to job applicants, except that if you already have a job you cannot even be required to *take* the medical examination unless it can be demonstrated that it relates to the job. (All applicants can be forced to take medical exams; an applicant with a disability cannot be excluded unless the results show something job-related.)

If the results reveal the existence of a disease that is a threat to your health or to the health of others, you can be fired only if the threat is a "significant risk of substantial harm . . . that cannot be eliminated or reduced by a reasonable accommodation." You cannot be fired because of fear of a contagious disease that is not a direct threat.

Even labor unions are covered by the ADA, and they have the same obligations to comply with its requirements. Although the terms of a union contract may be used to determine if reassignment to a vacant position is an undue hardship to the employer, the employer cannot use the union to take illegal action. For example, if the terms of a union contract contain physical requirements for employees that screen out people with disabilities and are not job-related and consistent with business necessity, they would violate the ADA.[31]

Problems often arise when employers do not obey the law, and no one expects the ADA to be implemented and accepted by every employer overnight. Although some of the predictions of "years of costly litigation" may have been overstated, everyone expects some employers to violate the requirements of Title I, either inadvertently or intentionally. You should know how to protect yourself against discrimination and illegal conduct.

H ow To Establish a Discrimination Case

Part of protecting yourself from illegal discrimination involves simply knowing the law and insisting that its requirements be followed. When this proves insufficient, it sometimes becomes necessary to take court or administrative action to rectify an illegal situation.

This can mean a formal lawsuit or simply a complaint to state or federal authorities. In either event, you must be prepared to prove illegal conduct; the American court system presumes innocence in criminal cases and, although the presumptions vary in civil discrimination matters, proving one's case is always essential.

Employment discrimination cases can be very difficult to prove. The central issue often is whether the employer fired an employee because of prejudice about the employee's disability or for a different reason that may be legal. Therefore, the employer's reasons and state of mind are important factors that are usually disputed. Because employers usually deny illegal motives, employees who have suffered discrimination should be very careful to document all illegal conduct and any indications of illegal motives.

Here are some general guidelines you may follow if you suspect that you are suffering discrimination because of a disability:

1. *Get it in writing.* The first rule you should follow is to get everything possible in writing. From the first year of law school, most lawyers are taught to "get it in writing," because written documents tend to "lock in" opponents to their position. If a supervisor refuses to provide a requested accommodation, try to get that supervisor, or his or her secretary, assistant, or another person, to write down the refusal. Failing this, you can always write a letter or memo confirming what occurred, what your physical or mental limitations were, and what you requested.

2. *Get witnesses for what you cannot get in writing.* Sometimes it is impossible to obtain everything in writing. For example, your supervisor may make oral comments that he or she would never commit to paper. In this instance, try to locate witnesses who can later testify to the statements. You can sometimes get the witnesses to write notes, a memo, or

a letter about what they heard. Such documents are helpful because they tend to lock in the person signing the note or memo to later testimony consistent with what he or she signed. Remember that some of your coworkers may overhear comments that are flagrantly illegal. If you later sue the employer, that "friend" can be put under tremendous pressure by the firm to simply "forget" them.

3. *A picture is worth a thousand words.* If there are things that can be photographed, take pictures. For example, if your job is inaccessible, take a roll of film and document the situation. Keep the negatives. Graphic photographs are very effective in a courtroom; the negatives from your camera can be blown up into posters or slides that may fascinate a jury tired of hearing endless testimony and looking at thousands of documents. If you need a special device as an accommodation, photograph it. You could even photograph its price tag! If you cannot walk and were carried up the stairs to a company party, have someone take a picture of that as well.

4. *Start from the beginning.* Keep a scrapbook of clippings, including the hiring advertisements, job descriptions, copies of the application and testing forms, and all of the initial paperwork. If you know the name of the person you are replacing, write down his or her name and address so you will know where to contact that person in the future.

5. *Do not lose things!* Keep your scrapbook throughout your job. You can keep the names and addresses of coworkers who may later leave the company, and you should definitely keep all notes, memos, and letters regarding your situation. Keep your employer's annual stockholder reports to show its size and the number of employees; this can be very important if your employer uses the undue hardship defense.

6. *It is especially important to keep all of your job evaluations and commendations.* In cases of illegal firing, employers tend to claim that termination was for poor work performance. If that is untrue, you should be able to prove it. However, your employer may happen to "lose" your glowing evaluations or commendations after you file a lawsuit.

7. *Keep a copy of your entire personnel file.* Request updates

regularly. Sometimes it can be very difficult to get a copy after termination, and it may be impossible to get a lawyer or government agency to help you unless you have evidence to back your position.

8. *Keep bound notebooks or diaries rather than "drop-in" files.* It is much easier to lose pages when they are not bound.

9. *Keep a copy of your company's personnel policy handbook.* Most large companies maintain elaborate personnel policies. Many of them have been recently amended to incorporate the provisions of Title I. It is sometimes helpful in a court case to catch a company violating its own policies; it is often more helpful to find the policies themselves illegal!

10. *Keep medical records to document your disability.* This seems basic, but you should be prepared to show that you are "a qualified individual with a disability" so you can prove that you qualify for protection by the ADA. Make sure the records are dated. If your situation fluctuates or changes, a diary of the interplay between your impairment and the accommodations offered at work can be helpful.

11. *Remember that your employer is under no obligation to provide a reasonable accommodation until he has been notified of your disability.* If you have a "hidden" disability, keep a dated copy of letters to your supervisor and the personnel department informing them of your need for accommodation.

12. *When things go wrong, do not delay!* Procrastination is the enemy of the successful litigant. Not only do memories of crucial witnesses fade, but the law is full of rules that require litigants to move quickly into court or administrative proceedings. These rule are called "statutes of limitations." If you delay until after the expiration of a statute of limitations, your case is forever barred. Even if you feel emotionally devastated or incapable of fighting back after a humiliating termination, seek an attorney as soon as possible. You may even consult one before termination, when you first suspect something illegal is going on.

13. *After termination, keep documenting your attempts to find another job.* Keep notes, ad clippings, and a diary. You may need to show that you lost wages as a result of an illegal firing, so you must be able to demonstrate that you diligently tried to find other suitable work. Document any visits to

outplacement counselors, employment agencies, and psychotherapists; you will need to prove how much you were hurt mentally and emotionally by the wrongful conduct.

In conclusion, remember that lawyers are not magicians. They cannot manufacture cases or conjure evidence that has been lost or destroyed. A lawyer is only as good as his or her case.

If you follow the preceding rules, you stand a much better chance of winning a discrimination suit or even of preventing illegal action from occurring. If you cannot prevent illegal conduct from occurring, you may have to pursue administrative action with state or federal authorities or file a lawsuit. If you prove your case, your employer can be penalized.

P enalties for Employment Discrimination

Employers who discriminate against people with disabilities run great risks. If you have suffered discrimination, you can take action against the employer in court or in administrative proceedings with the EEOC or other state agencies in your specific state.

The procedure for enforcing the ADA begins with filing a complaint with the EEOC. You can file the complaint in person, by telephone, or by mail, but the advice to "get it in writing" also applies here. You should be certain to file all complaints in writing and to get file-stamped copies to prove the filing date. You can call the EEOC to get the complaint form, but you should then file it in writing and send in an extra copy with a self-addressed envelope so that you get a file-stamped copy back. File the complaint long before any deadline expires.

Unless your EEOC complaint is filed within 180 days after the discriminatory act, the statute of limitations will expire. If you are still employed while suffering discrimination, you will legally be protected from retaliation by your employer. The actual procedures that follow the filing of the complaint are discussed in more detail in Chapter 9. However, you should know that if the EEOC does not take action or resolve the situation to your satisfaction, you are allowed to file suit in court.

Penalties for violating the ADA include reinstatement of a job, loss of back pay, injunctive relief (a court order to end discrimination), and compensatory or punitive damages (money). The monetary amounts available under the ADA for intentional discrimination are limited, depending on the size of the employer. The following schedule limits the amounts that can be awarded to compensate people for intentional violations of the ADA:

Number of Employees	Damages Cannot Exceed
15–100	$ 50,000
101–200	$100,000
201–500	$200,000
500 or more	$300,000

The amounts of damages are not limited in many of the states that prohibit disability discrimination, so your lawyer may want to sue under state law rather than under the ADA. Since this can get rather complicated, the best advice is to remember that employers can be severely punished for discriminating, but that you should not delay if you suffer discrimination. You should immediately contact a lawyer who is knowledgeable in this field to enforce your rights.[32]

These monetary amounts are maximums; no one should ever file a lawsuit hoping to get rich or expecting large monetary recoveries. Lawsuits are for people who have suffered discrimination, and large awards are rare. Use the courts only if you need them, and avoid administrative proceedings if you can.

S ummary

The most important protections provided by disability rights laws are those relating to employment protections. Different laws protect people with disabilities from job discrimination at state, local, and federal levels. The ADA is the most comprehensive nationwide series of laws, and its provisions go beyond merely outlawing discrimination. They actually require employers to provide reasonable accommodations for people with disabilities.

These "reasonable accommodations" can include almost anything that enables a person with a disability to perform the essential functions of a job. Accessible work sites, flexible schedules, and special devices are only a few of the things employers may be required to provide.

The employer's obligation to provide "reasonable accommodations" is tempered by the limitation that "undue hardships" to the firm are not required. This takes into account the size and financial resources of the employer. Larger businesses are required to spend more than smaller ones to accommodate employees with disabilities. No employer is required to change the essential nature of its operation.

To qualify for the right to a "reasonable accommodation" that does not impose an "undue hardship," you must be a "qualified individual with a disability." This requires that you (1) have all of the qualifications necessary for the job, such as education, credentials, and licenses; and (2) are able to perform the "essential functions" of the job if you are accommodated. These essential functions are the fundamental duties of the job, not marginal functions that really are not necessary.

If you are a qualified individual with a disability, you are entitled to equal treatment and reasonable accommodations from the beginning of the application process through to enjoyment of equal benefits and equal treatment in promotion, discipline, or termination. You cannot legally suffer discrimination on the basis of disability in any aspect of the employment process.

Employers who discriminate illegally risk severe penalties, and you should keep an accurate record of any illegal acts that you suffer. If you do so, you can act to receive the many benefits of Title I of the ADA.

R eferences

1. The definition of an employer covered by the ADA is found at 42 U.S.C.A. § 12111(5)(A) (West 1992).
2. The source for the statement that forty-five states already provided some job protections for people with disabilities is Sheryl E. Stein, *The Americans With Disabilities Act,* L.A. LAW, Sept. 1991, at 32.
3. The requirement of providing reasonable accommodation is found at 42 U.S.C.A. § 12112(b)(5)(A).
4. The quote about deliberate vagueness is from Steven F. Stuhlbarg, *Reasonable Accommodation Under the Americans With Disabilities Act: How Much Must One Do Before Hardship Turns Undue?,* 59 U. CINN. L. REV. 1311, 1326 (1991).
5. The list of items that may be included as reasonable accommodations is from 42 U.S.C.A. § 12111(9). The explanations from 29 C.F.R. app. § 1630.2(o) (1992) are included, as well as the examples from

the Equal Employment Opportunity Commission, Technical Assistance Manual, Part III (1992) [hereinafter EEOC Manual].

6. The parts of the EEOC regulations that define "reasonable accommodation" appear at 29 C.F.R §§ 1630.2(o), app. 1630.2(o) and 56 Fed. Reg. 35726, 35729 (1991). All comments and quotes from these regulations are taken from these three sources.

7. The four-step process of interaction to discuss reasonable accommodations was taken from the EEOC Manual, *supra* note 5, § 3.8 at III-9 to III-10.

8. The example of the guide dog is from 29 C.F.R. app. § 1630.2(o).

9. The examples of the employee lunchroom and deep pile carpeting are from the EEOC Manual, *supra* note 5, § 3.4 at III-3 to III-5.

10. The example of the blind security guard is from 29 C.F.R. app. § 1630.2(o). *See Coleman v. Darden,* 595 F.2d 533 (10th Cir. 1979).

11. The quote from Thurgood Marshall about balancing the two opposing concerns is from *Alexander v. Choate,* 469 U.S. 287, 299 (1985), addressing the question of if §504 of the 1973 Rehabilitation Act encompassed all claims of disparate-impact discrimination.

12. The ADA definition of undue hardship is found at 42 U.S.C.A. § 12111(10).

13. The EEOC regulations regarding the undue hardship definition and the example regarding the fast-food franchise is from 29 C.F.R. app. § 1630.2(p).

14. The examples of the employee pitching in $500, the waitress in the nightclub, the thermostat, the temporary construction site, the reassignment, the morale and the person on kidney dialysis treatment are from the EEOC Manual, *supra* note 5, § 3.9 at III-14 to III-16.

15. The quotes about the bleak outlook, deep resentment, and backwash of bitterness and the statements about Massachusetts, Virginia, and North Carolina law are from Stuhlbarg, *supra* note 4, at 1339-40.

16. The estimates of accommodation costs come from Jeffrey O. Cooper, *Overcoming Barriers to Employment: The Meaning of Reasonable Accommodation and Undue Hardship in the Americans With Disabilities Act,* 139 U. PA. L. REV. 1423, 1448-49 (1991).

17. The quotes of the ADA critics are from the articles by Stuhlbarg, *supra* note 4, at 1336-37, and Cooper, *supra* note 16, at 1450.

18. The ADA definition of qualified individual with a disability is from 42 U.S.C.A. § 12111(8). The following quote about satisfying the job's requisite skill and experience is from 29 C.F.R. § 1630.2(m).

19. The examples of the typist, the maid, the CPA, and the lawyer are from 29 C.F.R. app. §§ 1630.2(m)-1630.9.

20. The quote about the purpose of the second step of analysis for determining essential job functions is from 29 C.F.R. app. § 1630.2(n).

21. The three examples of essential job functions are from the EEOC Manual, *supra* note 5, § 2.3(a) at II-13 to II-14. The three categories are from 29 C.F.R. § 1630.2(n).

22. The four examples of essential and nonessential job functions are from the EEOC Manual, *supra* note 5, § 2.3(a) at II-13 to II-18.
23. The seven types of evidence are found at 29 C.F.R. § 1630.2(n). The examples mixed in with them are from the EEOC Manual, *supra* note 5, § 2.3(a) at II-13 to II-18.
24. The example of the applicant with dyslexia is from the EEOC Manual, *supra* note 5, § 3.10(7) at III-29.
25. The example about the TDD for the deaf person is from the EEOC Manual, *supra* note 5, §§ 5.2-5.3, at V-2 to V-3.
26. The employer's limitation to questions concerning the ability to do a job is from 29 C.F.R. § 1630.14(a). The statement about the exception for federal contractors is from the EEOC Manual, *supra* note 5, § 5.5(c) at V-8 to V-9.
27. The limitations on preemployment medical examinations are found at 42 U.S.C.A. 12112(d) and 29 C.F.R. § 1630.14. The wording about the risks of health as a reason for job refusal is from 29 C.F.R. § 1630.2(r). The statement about drug testing is from 29 C.F.R. § 1630.16(c). The example of the person with epilepsy is from the EEOC Manual, *supra* note 5, § 6.4 at VI-9.
28. The statement about the accommodation in testing and the quote about its purpose are from the EEOC Manual, *supra* note 5, § 5.6 at V-18 to V-19.
29. The discussion of equality in advancement, compensation training, evaluations, discipline, and discharge was taken from the EEOC Manual, *supra* note 5, §§ 7.5–7.8 at VII-5 to VII-8.
30. The discussion of insurance benefits is taken from 29 C.F.R. app. § 1630.5 and the EEOC Manual, *supra* note 5, § 7.9 at VII-8 to VII-10.
31. The discussion of medical testing and the direct threat standard is from 29 C.F.R. §§ 1630.2(r) and 1630.14(c).
32. The 180 day time limit and process of EEOC filing procedures is from the EEOC Manual, *supra* note 5, § 10 at X-1 to X-9.

four

Public Access

"The ADA means access to jobs, public accommodations, government services, public transportation and telecommunications - in other words, full participation in, and access to all aspects of society."
—*Foreword to the ADA Title III Technical Assistance Manual, by the U.S. Dept. of Justice.*

Titles II and III of the five-part Americans With Disabilities Act (ADA) deal with public access. These provisions require private businesses and the government to make public accommodations such as offices, restaurants, and stores usable by patrons with disabilities. Title II controls places and facilities run by governments and government agencies; Title III deals with public places operated by private businesses.

Although neither governments nor private businesses can discriminate against people with disabilities, the deadlines and rules for government-run facilities (Title II) and privately owned establishments (Title III) are different. Both Titles are intended to allow people with disabilities to take full part in American society. All *new construction* must comply with specific ADA guidelines. *Existing* buildings and services must be changed if such changes do not impose unreasonable burdens on the business or government agency.

Like many of the other parts of the ADA, the new accessibility requirements are controversial. Soon after the Act was passed, one representative claimed that ADA "horror stories" had *already* started to occur, and he claimed that the ADA would have "perverse and unintended results."[1]

Despite such dire predictions, the ADA's accessibility provisions do not yet appear to be destructive to American businesses. This is because existing public places that are owned by private businesses need only be made accessible for people with disabilities if the accessibility modifications are "readily achievable." Changes are not required unless they are "easily accomplishable without much difficulty or expense."

To fully understand the accessibility provisions of the ADA, you should understand:

1. the definition of "public accommodation";
2. the definition of what is "readily achievable";
3. what is required of private businesses;
4. what is required of government entities; and
5. what you should do if you believe your rights to access have been violated.

W hat Is a "Public Accommodation?"

Because the intent of the ADA's public accessibility rules is to give people with disabilities "full participation" in society, private businesses must make their *public areas* accessible to people with disabilities.

Title III contains a lengthy definition of "public accommodation"[2] as a facility that: (a) affects commerce; and (b) falls within at least one of the following twelve categories:

1. hotels, motels, inns, or other places of lodging (except for owner-occupied establishments that rent fewer than six rooms);
2. restaurants, bars, and other establishments that serve food or drink;
3. motion picture houses, theaters, concert halls, stadiums, or other places of exhibition or entertainment;
4. auditoriums, convention centers, lecture halls, or other places of public gathering;
5. bakeries, grocery stores, clothing stores, hardware stores, shopping centers, or other sales or rental establishments;
6. service establishments such as laundromats, dry cleaners, banks, barber shops, beauty shops, professional offices, lawyers' offices, hospitals, doctors' offices, and so on;
7. public transportation terminals, depots, or stations (not including air transportation faculties);
8. museums, libraries, galleries, or other places of public display or collection;
9. parks, zoos, amusement parks, or other places of recreation;
10. schools and other places of education;
11. social service centers such as day-care centers, senior citizen centers, homeless shelters, food banks, and adoption agencies; and
12. gymnasiums, health spas, bowling alleys, golf courses, and other places of exercise or recreation.[3]

In order for a facility to be considered a public accommodation, it must fall within at least one of these twelve categories. However, the examples given are only illustrations of what is included in each category. "For example, the category 'sales or rental establishments' would include many facilities other than those specifically listed, such as video stores, carpet showrooms and athletic equipment stores."[4]

Businesses are only required to make their *public* areas accessible. Areas where only employees go need not be accessible for use by the general public. For example, if a food processing company grows produce and supplies its crops only to food processors on a wholesale basis, it is not a "public accommodation" because it does not deal with the public. However, if the "company operates a roadside stand where its crops are sold to the public, the roadside stand would be a sales establishment covered by the ADA."[5]

Both the landlord who owns a building that contains a public accommodation and the tenant who owns or operates it are subject to the accessibility requirements of the ADA. Between them, they can decide who will pay for the necessary changes, but they are both legally responsible.[6]

Some groups are exempt from the provisions of Title III:

- Religious establishments such as churches and synagogues are exempt from the public access requirements of the ADA. For example, parochial schools that teach religious doctrine and day-care centers operated by religious organizations are exempt. However, if the congregation rents its facilities to a private day-care center or elementary school, the tenant is exempt only if it is also a religious establishment.
- Private clubs are exempt from the public access provisions of the ADA. Since it is often difficult to determine what is a "private club," courts usually find private club status when: (1) members exercise a high degree of control over club operations; (2) there is a highly selective process for accepting members; (3) substantial membership fees are charged; (4) the establishment is nonprofit; and (5) the club was not founded for the purpose of avoiding civil rights laws.[7]
- Commercial facilities such as oil refineries or meat packing plants, which are not public accommodations, need to comply with the ADA's accessibility provisions only when building *new* facilities or *remodeling*. They need not change existing facilities unless they are public accommodations.

With these few exceptions, all public accommodations covered by Title III must change their *existing* public areas to make them usable by people with disabilities. Wheelchair ramps, braille elevator keys, and handicapped parking spaces are a few of the modifications that might be required.

Public accommodations operated by private businesses are required to make their existing public areas accessible only if doing so is "readily achievable." This means that businesses are not required to make *every* change necessary to provide access to people with disabilities. The definition of "readily achievable" is crucial, since it determines the need to make changes in existing public places operated by private businesses.

What Does the "Readily Achievable" Standard Mean?

The ADA defines the term *readily achievable* as "easily accomplishable and able to be carried out without much difficulty or expense." However, it does not give explicit guidelines to determine what is "easily accomplishable" or what is considered substantial "difficulty or expense." Instead, as with the employment provisions of Title I, the ADA gives general guidelines that consider the financial resources of the specific private businesses that might have to make the proposed alterations.

In determining if an action is readily achievable, the ADA uses the same four factors that are used in Title I to determine what constitutes an "undue hardship" for employers. These are:

"(A) the nature and cost of the action needed . . . ;
(B) the overall financial resources of the facility involved . . . ;
(C) the overall financial resources of the covered entity; the overall size of the business with respect to the number of its employees; the number, type and location of its facilities; and
(D) the type of operation involved. . . . "[8]

The "readily achievable standard is a 'limitation' on the obligation to remove barriers" that bar people with disabilities from entering or using public facilities. It takes into account a wide range of factors and considers the fact that many local facilities are owned or operated by parent corporations that conduct operations at many different sites.[9]

Larger businesses with greater financial resources are required to make greater changes than smaller ones that cannot afford as much. The "readily achievable" standard that applies to private businesses is applied on a "case-by-case" basis since the Department of Justice left the crucial standard flexible. There is no numerical formula for determining if a proposed modification is "readily achievable." Cost, safety, crime prevention, and the finances of a business are considered in the "case-by case" approach.[10]

What Is Required of Private Businesses?

Title III basically requires that people with disabilities have access to all public accommodations operated by private businesses. This includes altering existing buildings if "readily achievable," building new ones in accessible ways, and making public programs available to people with disabilities. Businesses open to the public must also offer their goods and services in an integrated setting and cannot exclude individuals with disabilities from the full and equal enjoyment of their benefits.

The old "separate but equal" standard that was long since found illegal for racial segregation is also illegal for people with disabilities. Section 12182 requires that people with disabilities have equal opportunities to participate in all of the goods, services, facilities, privileges, and advantages offered by privately owned businesses to the public at large; these opportunities must be offered in the most integrated setting appropriate to the needs of people with disabilities. This is because a "primary goal of the ADA is the equal participation of individuals with disabilities into the 'mainstream' of American society."[11] The specific applications of this goal are best illustrated by examples.

- Museums cannot exclude blind people from tours because of assumptions about their ability to appreciate and benefit from the experience. Deaf people cannot be excluded from concerts. However, a museum can offer special additional tours for the blind, which blind people could *choose* to attend at their option.
- A museum can offer discount tickets for people with disabilities, but a disabled person can choose to pay the full rate and cannot be forced to accept the discount.
- Restaurants and other public places can neither refuse to serve people with disabilities nor seat them in special areas. Even limitations in insurance coverage do not justify exclusion; if an amusement park excludes individuals who do not meet a certain height requirement because its insurance does not cover the shorter people, the exclusion is illegal.
- Legitimate safety concerns based on "direct threats" of harm *are* sufficient bases for excluding people with disabilities.

For example, a white-water rafting tour company can exclude people who cannot swim. If the amusement park's height policy is justified by a direct safety threat rather than a mere insurance exclusion, the policy is legal.

- Places of public accommodation located in private homes are subject to the accessibility rules of Title III. That part of the home used by the public must comply. For example, a family home that uses some of its rooms for a day-care center must make those specific rooms accessible if this is "readily achievable."[12]

In conclusion, eligibility standards that tend to screen out people with disabilities or to deny them equal participation are illegal unless they are necessary for safety reasons. For example, a garage cannot refuse to accept vans if it has adequate roof clearance, since this would exclude mobility impaired people.

Barrier Removal in Existing Businesses

New buildings and buildings that are substantially remodeled are required to meet the complex accessibility guidelines for people with disabilities. The guidelines regulate doorway width, aisle width, toilet height, and even the height of automatic teller machines. Although this will have a gradual impact on society as more and more buildings are built or remodeled, it is already required in many states. For example, California's Administrative Code Title 24 has long set out guidelines for accessibility of publicly used structures; many other states and municipalities have similar rules.[13]

The ADA also requires a wide variety of modifications in *existing* public accommodations. Wheelchair ramps, wider doorways, and accessible toilets are only a few of the things that are required by the ADA if they are readily achievable.

The ADA only requires *readily achievable* modifications, and businesses need only make modifications that are "easily accomplishable and able to be carried out without much difficulty or expense." Explaining the specific application of this doctrine requires a study of the government's priorities and then a look at specific examples of what might be required.

The Department of Justice urges public businesses to comply with the barrier removal requirements of Title III in the following order of priorities: First, take measures to provide access so that people with disabilities can get into the place of business; examples include entrance ramps, wider doorways, or wider parking spaces. Second, provide accessible routes through the public areas of the business; this might include rearranging display racks or providing braille signage and visual alarms. Third, provide access to rest rooms. Fourth, take "any other measures necessary" to provide access to the goods, services, privileges, and advantages of the public business.[14]

Specific examples of what may be required to comply with the barrier removal provisions of Title III include:

- Installing wheelchair ramps if this is readily achievable for the specific business involved. Ramping a single step is usually considered readily achievable, and ramping several steps might be required in many circumstances. However, ramping an entire flight of stairs would seldom be necessary, since the readily achievable standard does not require extensive remodeling or burdensome expense.[15]
- Making curb cuts in sidewalks may be required if they are readily achievable.
- Repositioning shelves, tables, chairs, vending machines, furniture, telephones, and display racks may be required. This is considered readily achievable if there is no "significant loss of selling or serving space."[16]
- Installing flashing alarm lights for hearing impaired people may be required, as may be the installation of raised braille markings for elevator control buttons.
- Widening doors, installing offset door hinges to allow wheelchair clearance, eliminating turnstiles, and adding accessible door hardware may be required to help meet the first priority of providing access to facilities.
- Installing raised toilet seats, full-length mirrors, and grab bars in toilet stalls may be required to provide access to rest room facilities. It may even be necessary to rearrange toilet partitions, reposition paper towel dispensers, install accessible paper cup dispensers, and insulate pipes under sinks to prevent burns.

- Removal of high pile, low density carpeting may be necessary, if this is readily achievable, as this type of carpeting can be difficult for wheelchair users.[17]

The standard that must be applied to determine if each of these examples is legally required is the "readily achievable" one defined previously. If a modification is not costly or extensive and the business can easily afford it, it is likely to be considered readily achievable.

A modification that would make a business's services accessible is not legally mandated if it is *not* readily achievable. However, the business still needs to take alternative measures.

Alternatives to Barrier Removal

If barrier removal is not readily achievable, public accommodations must make their goods and services available through alternative methods if such methods are readily achievable. An alternative method is only considered when the public business can demonstrate that the removal of a barrier is not readily achievable. This is a sort of "last resort," since businesses first must consider removing the barriers that block access for people with disabilities.

Public accommodations may not charge extra for the use of alternative measures. Surcharges are not allowed, even to recover the cost of the alternative measure provided.

Examples of alternative measures that businesses may use include:

- A pharmacy that is inaccessible may choose to provide home delivery or curb service for people with disabilities.
- A video rental store that has high shelves which it cannot lower without a significant loss of selling space may choose to offer the service of its employees to retrieve the movies on the high shelves.
- A gas station may choose to offer its full-service gasoline at self-service prices rather than make its self-service pumps accessible. However, if the gas station has a single cashier in a security booth, the cashier need not leave the booth. Legitimate safety concerns may make the alternative not readily achievable.

- If making all screens accessible is not readily achievable, multiscreen cinemas may choose to establish film rotation schedules so that people who use wheelchairs can see all films at the cinema.
- Examinations and tests must be made available, and they must be offered in ways that accurately reflect an individual's aptitude or achievement level. For example, bar examiners may choose to provide readers for blind applicants; oral examinations may be offered in written form to people with hearing impairments.

These examples show some of the alternatives that businesses may offer to comply with the access requirements of the ADA if barrier removal is not readily achievable. The requirement of removing barriers or providing alternatives applies to all privately owned public accommodations. The requirements for publicly owned public accommodations are different.

W hat Is Required of Publicly Owned Facilities?

Public accommodations that are publicly owned are controlled by Title II of the ADA. Its provisions state that people with disabilities shall not be excluded from participation in the benefits of the services, programs, or activities of a public entity because of their disabilities.

Since the federal government and all recipients of federal aid are already covered by the Rehabilitation Act of 1973, the major impact of Title II is that it now extends the protection of the ADA to all state and local governments and to all of their departments and agencies. They may not discriminate on the basis of disability, and they must make their facilities accessible.

Existing publicly owned facilities are required to be made accessible in the same ways as privately owned accommodations. However, the standard for government accommodations is different from that for privately owned facilities.

Public entities are not required to make all their existing facilities accessible, but they are required to make all programs accessible unless it would "result in a fundamental alteration in the nature of the program or in undue financial and administrative burdens." This is intended to be a higher burden than the "readily achievable" burden placed on private businesses; publicly owned accommodations are expected to do more than private businesses to make existing facilities accessible.[18]

The public entity has the burden of proving that a proposed alteration would fundamentally alter the service involved or result in undue financial and administrative burdens. If so, the public entity has the responsibility to take other action to ensure that people with disabilities can receive its services and benefits.[19]

For example, governments are not required to destroy the essential nature of a historic property to make its rest rooms accessible, but basic access is required if it would not threaten the historic significance of the property.

Many of the provisions of Title II involve public transportation systems. Public entities that operate fixed-route systems, in which vehicles follow a prescribed route on a fixed schedule, can buy *new* vehicles only if they can be used by individuals with disabilities (including people who use wheelchairs). If *used* vehicles are purchased or leased, the entity must make "good faith efforts" to acquire accessible used vehicles. Governments operating these fixed-route systems must also provide paratransit services (such as special vehicles) usable by people with disabilities who cannot board the regular buses, unless the government provides only commuter buses. Any transportation system that is not a fixed-route system is considered a "demand-responsive system," and public entities that operate such systems buying new vehicles can buy only accessible ones.

The "one-car-per-train rule" requires all publicly operated train systems containing two or more vehicles to have at least one of the vehicles accessible to individuals with disabilities. This requirement will be gradually phased in, taking full effect no later than July 26, 1995. Historic trains need not be altered if modifications would significantly alter the historic character of the vehicle. Train stations must also be made accessible, but these provisions will also be phased in slowly. For example, existing intercity rail stations are to be made accessible as soon as possible, but they are not absolutely required to be so until July 26, 2010.[20]

In summary, all publicly and privately owned public places must comply with the accessibility rules of the ADA. New and remodeled structures are subject to strict accessibility guidelines;

existing public programs and facilities must make alterations that are not unduly burdensome. However, many businesses, and even many state and local governments, have ignored the new requirements of the ADA, violating the access rights of millions of Americans.

W hat Should You Do
If Your Access Rights Are Violated?

If you believe that your rights to public access have been violated, you should immediately begin to gather photographs, records, and documents that prove the violation occurred. Then you should keep accurate records so that you can take effective action if you choose to pursue the matter. You might end up in a court case about the accessibility violation; even if you do not, you may want to prove that a violation has occurred so it will be eliminated and other people with disabilities are not hurt or excluded from public goods or services.

Here are some general guidelines to follow if you believe that your access rights have been violated:

1. Photograph the barrier(s) that restrict or prevent access. If a stair, aisle, or turnstile prevents your entry to a public accommodation, take pictures of it. Write down the date of the picture and the name of the photographer (you can take the pictures yourself). Photographic evidence can be the most important part of an accessibility lawsuit; it is often indisputable. Try to photograph the barrier from various angles so that the width of a doorway or aisle cannot be disputed. You may even want to include a yardstick in the picture if you can!

2. Take notes of what you wanted to buy or acquire at the facility involved and why you desired to go there in the first place. Date the notes and keep them to help you recall the circumstances of your visit.

3. Find out the name of the owner of the business and its size. This can be crucial since the application of the readily achievable standard varies depending on the size of the

business. In many instances, a simple phone call to determine the name of the business will do; in other circumstances, checking the public records of fictitious business names will be necessary in order to find out who really owns the accommodation.

4. Check the local records at your city or county building inspection department or permit bureau to determine if any major renovations have been performed at the accommodation's address. This can be the most important rule of all, since many state laws and parts of the ADA apply only to new or remodeled buildings. The local records of building permits often show when remodeling occurred and how much it cost.

5. Keep your medical records to show that you have a disability that restricted your access to the facility involved.

6. Do not lose things. Keep all photographs and records in one place so you can find them when you need them.

7. Never procrastinate. If you delay, your case can forever be barred because of strict rules (called "statutes of limitations") that require lawsuits and administrative complaints to be filed promptly. Seek help from a lawyer or government agency as soon as you can.

The enforcement procedures for accessibility violations involve administrative complaints to the Department of Justice and court lawsuits. If you file your own lawsuit under the ADA, you can obtain injunctive relief (an order correcting the violation) and attorney fees. However, you cannot recover monetary damages under the ADA unless the Attorney General takes your case. If the Attorney General sues, the court can award you money and can fine the offending business up to $50,000 for a first violation, $100,000 for any subsequent violation.[21]

Since the ADA does not allow monetary awards for private plaintiffs (the person suing for an access violation), it is imperative that you quickly seek help from an attorney experienced in disability rights cases as soon as you perceive that your access rights have been violated. The attorney may be knowledgeable about state law access requirements that can allow much greater rewards than the ADA.

S ummary

The ADA, as well as many state and local laws, requires that public accommodations be accessible to people with disabilities. The ADA's definition of "public accommodation" is broad; it encompasses all areas of businesses, governments, museums, and even parks that are used by the public.

Private businesses must build all new or remodeled buildings in ways that provide access for people with disabilities. They must also take action to make their existing facilities accessible if such action is "readily achievable," defined as "easily accomplishable without much difficulty or expense." The application of this standard varies with the cost of the proposed modification and the size of the business involved. If removal of a barrier is not readily achievable, the business must take alternative measures to make its goods or services available, if those measures are readily achievable.

Publicly owned public accommodations are also required to be accessible. Existing buildings must be made accessible unless it would result in a fundamental alteration in the nature of the public program or an undue financial or administrative burden. This imposes a higher burden on publicly owned facilities than the "readily achievable" standard used for privately owned public places. Governments are also required to make public transit fully accessible, with specific requirements that will be phased in over a period of years.

If your rights to access have been violated, you should photograph and document the situation and seek assistance from a knowledgeable lawyer or government agency as soon as possible. If you do, you can enjoy the full participation in American society that is promised by the ADA.

R eferences

1. Both the quotation about "perverse and unintended results" and the story about Mother Theresa are quoted from 136 CONG. REC. E2939 (daily ed. Sept. 21, 1990) (statement of Rep. Dannemeyer).
2. The quote about full participation is from 42 U.S.C.A. § 12101(a)(8) (West 1992).

3. 42 U.S.C.A. § 12181(7) (West 1992).
4. U.S. Department of Justice, The Americans With Disabilities Act, Title III Technical Assistance Manual, § III - 1.2000 at 2 [hereinafter DOJ Manual].
5. 28 C.F.R. Pt. 36, app. B § 36.104 (1992).
6. 28 C.F.R. § 36.201(b) (1992).
7. DOJ Manual, *supra* note 4, § III - 3.4000 at 5.
8. 42 U.S.C.A. § 12181(9).
9. 28 C.F.R. Pt. 36, app. B § 36.104.
10. 28 C.F.R. Pt. 36, app. B § 36.104.
11. The quote about the "primary goal of the ADA" is from DOJ Manual, *supra* note 4, § III - 3.4000 at 14.
12. The list of examples of what might be required of privately owned public accommodations such as museums, amusement parks, family day-care centers, etc., is from DOJ Manual, *supra* note 4, § III - 3.4100 to III - 4.1200 at 14–21.
13. The entire set of ADA Guidelines can be found at 28 C.F.R. Pt. 36, app. A. They are too lengthy to be discussed in detail in this text.
14. The priorities for removing barriers is found at 28 C.F.R. § 36.304(c) (1991).
15. The example about ramping a single step, several steps, or a whole flight is found at 28 C.F.R. Pt. 36, app. B § 36.304.
16. The quote about "significant loss of selling or serving space is from 28 C.F.R. Pt. 36, app. B § 36.304.
17. The list of examples of possibly required modifications is from 28 C.F.R. § 36.304(b).
18. The discussion of the standard for barrier removal in publicly owned public buildings, and the intent that the standard be higher for publicly owned than privately owned facilities is from 28 C.F.R. Pt. 35, app. A § 35.150 (1992).
19. 28 C.F.R. § 35.150(a).
20. The discussion concerning threatening historical significance of a building is from 28 C.F.R. Pt. 35, app. A § 35.150. The provisions about public transportation, the one-car-per-train rule, and train stations can be found at 42 U.S.C.A. §§ 12142–12148 (West 1992).
21. The enforcement provisions of the ADA and the punitive award limits are contained in 42 U.S.C.A. § 12188.

five

Insurance Problems

"Access to health insurance and health related services is extremely difficult to obtain for people with disabilities."
—*Sandra S. Parrino, quoted in National Council on Disability News Release, January 31, 1992.*

The American health care system is widely considered to be in a state of crisis, as witnessed by our government's strong focus on that area at the time of this writing (Spring 1993). Our country spends a larger percentage of its gross national product (GNP) on health care than any other industrial nation; 14 percent of our GNP was projected for health care costs in 1992 versus an average of 8.7 percent for many other industrialized countries. Yet our health care is no better than that of comparable nations. Approximately one in every seven Americans has no health insurance, and millions more have inadequate insurance.

Both able-bodied people and people with disabilities have problems with health care and health insurance. In fact, nine out of ten people surveyed in an August 1991 *Los Angeles Times* Gallup poll agreed that there is a health care crisis in our country. Eighty-five percent thought that America's health care system needed major reform.

Access to health care and health insurance is extremely limited for people with disabilities. Many private health insurance plans do not accept people with preexisting medical conditions, and plans that do cover such people often exclude the costs of such preexisting conditions. Since insurance is frequently tied to employment, the high percentage of people with disabilities who are unemployed means that there is also a high percentage of people with disabilities who lack adequate health insurance.

Obtaining life insurance and disability insurance can also be difficult for people with disabilities. Some insurance companies are reluctant to offer such policies to a great number of people whose conditions are not (or no longer) considered life-threatening.

There are some legal protections for people with disabilities who have insurance problems. The ADA offers limited protection for health, life, and disability insurance. Although it allows health insurance companies to exclude people with preexisting conditions, such conditions cannot be used as a "subterfuge" to evade the purposes of the ADA. State laws also offer some legal protections; some states require that insurance companies not deny coverage for people with disabilities without "valid actuarial data."

T he Impact of the ADA on Insurance

When the National Council on Disability first drafted the Americans With Disabilities Act, it included provisions related to health insurance that would have helped people with disabilities to obtain insurance. However, those provisions were later dropped. Congress was either reluctant to tackle the powerful insurance lobby or simply "battle-weary" after months of haggling over the key provisions of the ADA.

The final draft of the ADA included a section that allowed health insurance companies to continue "classifying risks." Insurance companies can continue "underwriting risks" (excluding people with preexisting medical conditions) unless it violates the law of the state involved. This section was added to the "miscellaneous" provisions of the ADA to protect insurance companies from the broad scope of the ADA after Congress dropped the provision that would have helped people with disabilities. However, this protection for insurance companies, which is somewhat convoluted, provides that it "shall not be used as a subterfuge to evade the purposes" of the ADA.[1]

The Equal Employment Opportunities Commission explained that the provision is "not intended to disrupt the current nature of insurance underwriting, or current insurance industry practices . . . even if they result in limitations on individuals with disabilities. . . ." However, insurers and employers cannot limit access to insurance coverage based on disability unless the disability poses *increased risks*.[2]

The Department of Justice concluded that "Congress intended to reach insurance practices by prohibiting differential treatment of individuals with disabilities . . . unless the differences are justified." Under the ADA, a person with a disability cannot be denied insurance unless his or her disability can be determined to pose increased risks. The classification of risks must be based on "sound actuarial principles or be related to actual or reasonably anticipated experience."[3]

The Americans With Disabilities Act therefore provides some protections for people with disabilities seeking insurance coverage, despite the provisions that allow insurance companies to continue "business as usual." Unfortunately, insurance companies can still "classify" and "underwrite" risks, meaning they can exclude people with preexisting medical conditions or charge them more for benefits. But denials must be based on "sound actuarial data" and exclusions cannot be used as a "subterfuge" to evade the purposes of the ADA.

T he Right To Be Excluded

The ADA allows insurance companies to continue "underwriting" risks. This means that insurance companies can continue their current practices of determining whether or not and on what basis an application for insurance will be accepted. Essentially, the ADA allows insurance companies to continue business as usual and to continue to exclude people with preexisting medical conditions.

A "preexisting condition" is a physical or mental condition that existed prior to issuance of an insurance policy. Most health insurance applications have lengthy questionnaires regarding the health of an applicant. Applicants are usually asked several questions about their health and about each doctor they have seen in the recent past. Insurance companies often contact these doctors to determine if applicants have preexisting conditions.

Insurance companies are allowed to deny the application of a person with a preexisting condition or to accept the application but exclude payments for medical costs related to that condition. Some critics have termed this "the right to be excluded." Insurance companies can exclude people with diabetes, HIV infection, or any other disease that increases the risk that the insurance company will have to pay for medical costs. As noted previously, the ADA's only protections for people with disabilities excluded from insurance coverage are the requirements that denials be based on "sound actuarial data" and not be used as a "subterfuge" to evade the purposes of the ADA.

The meaning of these terms is vague at best. The requirement that insurance companies use "sound actuarial data" means that they can only exclude conditions that can be determined to pose increased risk. In this era of rapid medical advances, many conditions that were once considered life-threatening or were very expensive to treat are no longer as risky. An insurance company may use an outdated medical text ten or twenty years old to support its claim that a specific condition imposes increased risks. Unless insurance laws change drastically within the next few years, one can expect that the meaning of the term *sound actuarial data* will be decided in court.

The meaning of the term *subterfuge* may also have to be decided in court. That word was defined by the Supreme Court to mean a "scheme, plan, stratagem or artifice of evasion." However, the Supreme Court was interpreting a different law when it gave that definition; it may have to decide if the same definition will be given to the word *subterfuge* as it is used in the ADA.[4]

The meaning of these two terms used to help people with disabilities is unclear. In fact, a legal newspaper stated: "If one thing is clear about the Americans With Disabilities Act, it is that the section dealing with health insurance is cloudy." People with disabilities have some rights to health insurance, but it may only be the right to be excluded from health insurance coverage.[5]

S tate Law Protections for People Seeking Insurance

Some states provide protections for people with disabilities seeking to obtain insurance. For example, California law provides that companies offering life, annuity, or disability insurance cannot limit coverage for people with disabilities unless the limitation is based on sound actuarial principles or related to actual and reasonably anticipated experience. California law also provides the same protection for people who are blind.[6]

These terms—*sound actuarial principles* and *actual and reasonably anticipated experience*—are similar to the terminology of the ADA. However, California law applies these terms to life, annuity, and disability insurance rather than to health insurance.

Other states have similar provisions protecting people with disabilities, which often provide that insurance limitations must be based on "sound actuarial data." This begs the question "What is sound actuarial data?" If you are denied insurance coverage and do not believe that there is a good reason for the denial, you should write to the insurance company and demand coverage. Usually the insurance company must provide the reason for your denial if you request it in writing. Retain a lawyer if necessary. Since the ADA and many state laws require that sound actuarial principles be applied, insurance companies cannot deny coverage without a good reason.

S uggestions for People with Insurance Problems

Since our health care system is in a state of crisis, and insurance coverage is often difficult to obtain, people with disabilities should be extremely careful when dealing with insurance companies. If you have insurance problems, you may want to consider the following suggestions:

- *Read the fine print.* Carefully read every word of advertising and fine print before buying *any* insurance policy, especially concerning preexisting conditions or other matters that concern you. Insurance policies are almost impossible to understand, so be careful and make sure every important term is explained to you. If you have any doubt, have the insurance representative put the company's interpretation in writing.
- *Get it in writing.* Remember that insurance law is a type of "contract" law, which means that the insurance company is bound only by its agreement with you. Make sure that any provisions you need are in writing. Question the insurance agent about preexisting conditions or other matters of concern, and insist that the agent point out specific written provisions of the policy.
- *Shop until you drop.* Insurance policies vary greatly. No two policies are exactly alike and comparisons are extremely difficult. The average family spends more on health insurance than on the purchase of a new car, so you should spend as much time shopping for insurance as you do test-driving new cars. *A wrong move with respect to health insurance for a person with a disability can mean financial disaster.*
- *Do not lie on applications.* If you are not honest on your insurance application, the insurance company can refuse to pay you the benefits of the policy. It can also rescind the policy long after you have been paying premiums.
- *Fight stupid decisions.* If an insurance company makes a decision denying coverage or benefits that you believe is not based on actual risks, you should contest the decision. Write a letter demanding an explanation of the reason for the denial. Hire a lawyer if necessary.

S ummary

Protections for people with disabilities seeking insurance are not clearly defined. The ADA and many states provide some protections, but most preexisting conditions can still be excluded from health insurance, and many of the protections for people with disabilities are couched in vague language that may have to be interpreted by courts.

Many of these problems will be resolved in the near future. Indeed, the entire American system of health care insurance may change drastically within the next several years. Until the necessary changes occur, life, health, and disability insurance will be difficult for people with disabilities to obtain.

R eferences

1. 42 U.S.C.A. Section 12201(c).
2. Appendix to 29 C.F.R. Section 1630.16(f), found at 56 F.R. 35753.
3. Section-by-Section Analysis in Response to Comments regarding 28 C.F.R. 36.212, found at Federal Register pages 35562-35563.
4. *Public Employees Retirement System of Ohio v.Betts,* 492 U.S. 158, 109 S.Ct. 2854, 106 L.Ed.z 134 (1989).
5. *San Francisco Recorder,* June 8, 1992.
6. California Insurance Code Sections 10144 and 10145.

six

What Government Benefits Are Available?

"The basic idea behind Social Security is a simple one. You pay taxes into the system during your working years, and you and members of your family receive monthly benefits when you retire or become disabled . . . .To get SSI, your income and the value of the things you own must be below certain limits . . . . Medicare is our country's basic health insurance program for people 65 or older and for many disabled people."

—*Understanding Social Security, by the Dept. of Health and Human Services, SSA Publication No. 05-10024, January 1992.*

Our federal government has three basic programs that benefit people with disabilities: Social Security, Supplemental Security Income, and Medicare. Each has a different purpose and different benefits for people with disabilities.

Social Security, a safety net for America's workers, is a type of insurance plan. Workers pay into the system during their working years and receive benefits when they retire or become disabled. Note that "disabled" for Social Security purposes requires that you be unable to perform any "substantial" work for at least a year.

Supplemental Security Income is available for people 65 or older or for people who are blind or disabled, who do not have a substantial income or many possessions. For example, as of 1992 a person was not eligible for SSI if he or she had possessions worth over $2,000; a couple could not get SSI with possessions valued at more than $3,000.

Medicare is a form of health insurance paid for with our Social Security taxes. Medicare pays for hospital benefits for people who are 65 or older or who are disabled. People entitled to receive Medicare can also acquire medical insurance for nonhospital medical care by paying a relatively small premium.

U nderstanding the Social Security Program

All workers pay a portion of their wages to the federal government for Social Security and Medicare. In 1992, each employee paid a tax of 7.65 percent of his or her gross salary, up to a limit of $55,500. Each employer made a matching contribution of 7.65 percent, so that 15.3 percent of each worker's wages up to $55,500 went to the Social Security system in 1992. Each self-employed person paid 15.3 percent of his or her taxable income up to the same limit.

Social Security benefits are not paid until you reach 65 years of age or become disabled. You can then collect the benefits if you have enough "credits" to be "insured."

As you work and pay taxes into the Social Security system, you earn Social Security "credits." Almost everyone who works earns four credits per year. In 1992, workers earned one credit for each $570 earned, up to a maximum of 4 credits per year. Most people need forty credits (ten years of work) to be "insured" and qualify for Social Security benefits.

People with disabilities under the age of 31 do not need forty credits to be "fully insured" for Social Security purposes. The number of work credits needed for disability benefits depends on your age when you become disabled.

- Before age 24—you need six credits in a three-year period ending when your disability starts.
- Ages 24–31—You need credit for having worked half the time between 21 and the time you become disabled. For example, if you became disabled at age 27, you would need credit for three years of work (out of six years).
- Ages 31 or older—You need to have the same number of work credits as you would need for retirement, as shown in the following chart. Also, you generally must have earned at least twenty of the credits in the ten years immediately before you became disabled.

Born After 1929, Become Disabled at Age	Born Before 1930, Become Disabled Before 62	Credits You Need
31–42		20
44		22
46		24
48		26
50		28
52		30
53		31
54		32
55		33
56		34
57	1986	35
58	1987	36
59	1988	37
60	1989	38
62 or older	1991 or later	40[1]

If you have earned enough credits to receive Social Security benefits, you are "fully insured" for Social Security purposes. However, you may receive the benefits only if you are 65 or older or if you become "disabled" within the meaning of the Social Security program.

S ocial Security's Definition of the Word *Disabled*

Disability under Social Security is based on one's inability to work. You are considered disabled if you have a physical or mental impairment that keeps you from performing any "substantial gainful work" and it is expected to last twelve months or result in death. A child is considered to be disabled if a disability affects his or her ability to do the things and behave in the ways that such a child normally would.

This definition of the word *disability* is very different from the ADA's definition and from the definition found in a dictionary. The Social Security Administration (SSA) determines if you are disabled by using a five-step process. The five questions are:

1. *Are you working?* If you are working and your earnings average more than $500 a month, you generally cannot be considered disabled.

2. *Is your condition "severe?"* Your impairment must significantly limit your physical or mental ability to perform "basic work activities." These include the ability to "walk, stand, sit, lift, carry, push, pull, reach, and handle as well as the capacity to see, hear, and speak. Mentally, basic work activities require the aptitude to understand, carry out, and remember simple instructions, to use judgment, to respond appropriately to supervisors, coworkers, and usual work situations, and to deal with changes in a routine work setting."[2]

3. *Is your condition found in the list of disabling impairments?* The Social Security Administration maintains a list of impairments for each of the major body systems that are considered severe. If your condition is not on the list, the Administration determines if it is of equal severity to an impairment that is on the list.

4. *Can you do the work you previously did?* The Social Security Administration considers the work that you did for a period of at least three months within the past fifteen years. Your claim will be denied if your condition is not severe enough to prevent you from doing any of that work. If it is sufficiently severe, your claim will be considered further.

5. *Can you do any other type of work?* If you cannot do the work you did in the last fifteen years, the Administration considers your age, education, past work experience, and transferable skills to decide if you can do any other type of work. Your claim will be approved if you cannot do any other kind of work.

The Social Security Administration considers these five questions in deciding if you are "disabled" within the meaning of their rules. Therefore, it is important that you not downplay your limitations or overstate your abilities when you apply for Social Security.

Applying for Social Security Benefits

You should apply for Social Security benefits as soon as you become disabled, since it takes at least sixty to ninety days for the Social Security Administration to process your claim. You can apply by phone, by mail, or in person at the nearest office. An SSA case worker fills out part of the application, and you fill in any missing information and sign the application. You must also furnish a W-2 tax form for the year prior to the onset of disability and a certified copy of your birth certificate.

When you apply for Social Security, you should understand that the claims process is "adversarial"; that is, you try to get benefits for yourself while the Administration tries to find reasons to deny them. You *must* be ready to prove your claim.

You can appeal the decision if your claim is denied or if you disagree with any other decision of the Social Security Administration. There are four levels of appeal. First, your claim is reconsidered and reviewed by people other than those who made the original decision. If you disagree with the reconsideration, you can appeal to the second level and may apply for a hearing before a judge. The third level of appeal is to the Appeals Council, which reviews your case if it believes that there is an issue that the judge did not address. If the Appeals Council denies your review, you can appeal to the United States District Court.

You have sixty days from the time you receive the decision to file an appeal to the next level. If a notification of a decision comes to you by mail, you have five days from the date of mailing before the sixty days begins to run, meaning that you have a total of sixty-five days from the date of mailing of a notice to file an appeal to the next level. Your appeal will be barred if you do not act within this time period

How Large Are the Benefits?

The amount of benefits that you will receive is based on your lifetime average earnings covered by Social Security. Obviously, the more you paid into Social Security, the more you will get back. The SSA keeps records of the amount of Social Security taxes paid by each person. To obtain an estimate of your benefits and how many quarters of coverage are credited to your account, call or write the nearest SSA office and ask that a form for requesting that information be mailed to you. If you fill out the form and send it to SSA, you will get a "Personal Earnings and Benefit Estimate Statement."

Summary of the Social Security Program

The Social Security program benefits people who have paid into the Social Security system. To obtain benefits, you must have worked a sufficient number of quarters to be "insured." If you have done so, you can collect benefits when you become disabled (that is, unable to work). The standards are strict, so you must be able to prove that you cannot do any "substantial" work for at least a year. The Social Security application process has all the hallmarks of an adversarial proceeding, so you should be careful not to downplay your functional limitations when you apply.

U nderstanding Supplemental Security Income

The term *supplemental security income* is a complete misnomer, since it is only available to people who do not have much other income or many assets.

SSI is available for people who are over 65, blind, or disabled. The standard for deciding if you are "disabled" is the same as that used to determine if you are disabled for Social Security purposes; it is based on your inability to work.

Before you can obtain SSI, you must meet certain criteria.

1. You must live in the United States or Northern Mariana Islands.
2. You must be a citizen of the United States or live in the United States legally.
3. If you are eligible for Social Security, you must apply for it. You can get benefits from both SSI and Social Security if you are eligible for both.
4. If you are disabled, you must accept vocational rehabilitation services if they are offered.
5. You must not own assets worth more than $2,000 (for a single person) or $3,000 (for a couple). However, this sum does not include the value of the home you live in, your car, burial plots, up to $1,500 in burial funds, and some household goods and life insurance policies.
6. You must not earn more than is allowed by the Administration rules, which differ depending on the state you live in. In order to obtain SSI, you must have a limited income, but the limit differs depending on the state in which you live. Call the Social Security office nearest you to find out what the limits are in your area. To determine your income, you do not count the first $20 per month of most income received; the first $65 from working, and half the amount over $65; food stamps; most food, clothing, or shelter you get from private nonprofit organizations; and most home energy assistance. If you work even though you are disabled, Social Security does not count wages that you use to pay for things you need because of your disability in order to work.[3]

Applying for SSI

You apply for SSI at the Social Security Administration office nearest where you live. You should take with you your Social Security card (or other evidence of the number), your birth certificate or other proof of your age, information about your home, payroll slips, bankbooks, and other documents showing what you own.

If you are signing up for disability, you should also bring the names, addresses, and telephone numbers of doctors, hospitals, and clinics where you have been treated.

You Do Not Need To Be "Insured"

SSI does not require that you be credited with a certain number of quarters of work. In this sense, you do not need to be "insured" as you would be to receive Social Security. SSI is a form of federal welfare available to people in financial need who meet strict tests to determine if they are disabled and who can prove that they are in need. You should be aware that you cannot receive both Aid for Families with Dependent Children and SSI. You must decide which of these two benefits to receive. However, you can receive both food stamps and SSI.

U nderstanding Medicare

Medicare is a form of national health insurance that is available to people who are over 65, blind, or disabled. It is available to people who are entitled to Social Security benefits. The same tests for deciding if you are entitled to receive Social Security apply in deciding if you can receive Medicare.

Medicare has two parts. The first part is "hospital insurance," which helps pay for inpatient hospital care, inpatient care in a skilled nursing facility, home health care, and hospice care. The second part is "medical insurance," which pays for certain doctor's charges and outpatient care.

Hospital Insurance

Medicare's hospital insurance is available to everyone in the Medicare program. Although it pays for many health care costs, its most important feature is inpatient hospital care.

Medicare hospital insurance helps pay for up to ninety days in any Medicare-participating hospital during each benefit period. Since most, but not all, hospitals participate in the Medicare program, you should check with the hospital before you are admitted, if you are able to do so. For the first sixty days of the hospital stay, Medicare hospital insurance pays for all covered services above a deductible amount. For days sixty-one through ninety, Medicare hospital insurance pays for all covered services except a daily deductible. A new benefit period begins if you are out of the hospital for at least sixty consecutive days and then return. If you need more than ninety days of inpatient care, you can decide to use some or all of your "reserve days," an extra sixty hospital days that are available if you have a long illness. *You have only sixty reserve days in your lifetime.*

Medicare hospital insurance pays for the following when you are in the hospital:

- semiprivate rooms and meals;
- nursing services;
- operating and recovery rooms;
- intensive care and coronary care;
- drugs, laboratory tests, and X-rays;
- medical supplies and appliances;
- rehabilitation, such as physical therapy; and
- some preparatory services.

Medicare hospital insurance also pays for similar types of services in skilled nursing facilities. It helps pay for up to one hundred days in any Medicare-participating skilled nursing facility in any benefit period. It pays for all covered services for the first twenty days, and for the next eighty days it pays for all services except a daily amount that you must pay. Covered services include meals, a semiprivate room, nursing, and physical therapy. The daily amount you pay is called "coinsurance."

If you are confined to your home and meet certain other conditions, Medicare can pay the full cost of home health visits from a Medicare-participating doctor or home health agency. There is no limit on the number of visits you can have.

Medicare hospital insurance also pays for hospice care for terminally ill people in Medicare-certified hospice facilities. For these, there is a maximum of two ninety-day periods, one thirty-day period, and one extension period of indefinite duration. Hospital insurance pays almost all of the costs of outpatient drugs and inpatient hospice care.

Medicare Medical Insurance

If you qualify for Medicare hospital insurance, you can also obtain Medicare medical insurance by paying a premium. Most people who have Medicare hospital insurance do pay the premium for medical insurance, since it is less than a private insurance company would charge. The premium changes from year to year, so you should contact the Social Security Administration to find out the current amount.

Medicare medical insurance pays for doctors' services, including:

- medical and surgical services;
- diagnostic tests that are part of your treatment;
- X-rays;
- radiology and pathology services;
- drugs that cannot be self-administered, blood transfusions, and other medical supplies;
- outpatient hospital services;
- ambulance transportation.;
- home dialysis equipment and support services; and
- radiation treatments.

Deductible. Like most other insurance policies, Medicare medical insurance requires that you pay a deductible in each year that it pays for services. After you pay the deductible, Medicare generally pays 80 percent of the approved charges for covered services for the rest of the year.

Medicare does not pay for *all* medical services. Some examples of what Medicare does not pay for are:

- dental care and dentures;
- routine checkups;
- immunization shots;
- most prescription drugs;
- eyeglasses and hearing aids;
- personal comfort items, such as a telephone or television in your hospital room;
- most nursing home care; and
- custodial care.[4]

Medicare Eligibility Requirements

Medicare is available to anyone who receives Social Security or Railroad Retirement benefits. It is also available if you are not receiving Social Security but you have worked long enough to be eligible for it, or if you are entitled to it based on your spouse's record and your spouse is at least 62 years old. It is also available to people who have worked long enough for federal, state, or local governments to be insured for Medicare.

Medicare is *not* available for people under the age of 65 unless they have been receiving Social Security disability benefits for at least twenty-four months, or unless they worked for a federal, state, or local government and meet the requirements of the Social Security disability program. If you are applying for Medicare because of your disability, it will not start until you have received Social Security disability benefits for twenty-four months.

Applying for Medicare

You apply for Medicare at the nearest Social Security Administration office. You must apply within seven months of becoming eligible. This seven-month period begins three months before the month you first become eligible and ends three months after that month. Therefore, *if you contemplate a need for Medicare, you should be very careful to apply within the enrollment period.*

If you do not sign up during the initial enrollment period but later change your mind, you are given another chance to sign up each year. This is the "general enrollment period," which runs from January 31 through March 31 of each year. However, if you enroll during the general enrollment period, Medicare coverage does not start until the following July.

R eferences

1. *Disability* by the U.S. Department of Health & Human Services, Social Security Administration, published by the Department of Health and Human Services, SSA Publication No. 05-10029, January 1992, pages 6 and 7.

2. "Social Security Disability Benefits: An Overview," by Bruce H. Swecker, J.D., *Connecticut Medicine,* December, 1991, Vol. 55, No. 12, page 708.
3. *SSI, Supplemental Security Income,* by the U.S. Department of Health & Human Services, Social Security Administration, SSA Publication No. 05-11000, Jan. 1992, pages 6–8.
4. *Medicare,* by the U.S. Department of Health & Human Services, Social Security Administration, SSA Publication No. 05-10043, January 1992, page 20.

seven

What Happens If I Die or Become Incapacitated?

"Intestacy. The state or condition of dying without having made a valid will, or without having disposed by will of a part of his property."
—*Black's Law Dictionary, 5th Ed., West Publishing Company, 1979.*

Most people are extremely reluctant to think about their own death or incapacitation. Since planning for the disposal of one's property after death or incapacitation requires *thinking* about it, many people do not make sufficient financial plans for their demise. However, everyone should make plans for their passing to avoid added pain and confusion for their loved ones.

The first thing you should do is *make a valid will*. If you die without a valid will, your property passes by the laws of "intestacy." This means that you have no control over the disposition of your property after you die; the laws of the state in which you lived determine who will receive it.

Each state has different laws governing the division of property for people who die intestate (without a valid will). In most states, your property is divided among your spouse and children. Some states may give fifty percent of your property to your surviving spouse, with fifty percent divided equally among your children, whereas others may give the major portion of your property to your children. If you have no spouse and no children, your parents and other close relatives generally are given your property after your death. If you have no heirs, your property usually is given to the state.

A *will*, which must be signed and witnessed, is a document that outlines how your property (your "estate") is to be distributed. The will appoints a person known as the "executor" to govern the distribution of your property. Some wills, known as "holographic" wills, are handwritten and not witnessed. They are not recommended because courts often do not find them valid. A will is the most common device that people use to control the disposition of their property after death.

The second most common device used for estate planning is the "trust," which is more complicated than a will and generally costs more to create. Trusts are gaining in popularity because they can sometimes reduce legal fees after you die.

If you worry about becoming incapacitated and wish to appoint someone else to make decisions about your finances and health care while you are alive but unable to make such decisions, you may desire a Durable Power of Attorney. This can be temporary (such as during an operation) or permanent, depending on how it is structured. Such a document gives another person the power to make decisions in financial or health care matters, or even the right to order that life support machines be discontinued in the event of complete incapacitation.

Since "none of us is getting out of here alive," we should all make plans for the disposal of our property after death. The three most common planning devices - wills, trusts, and durable powers of attorney - are discussed in the following sections.

W ills

A will is a document created to tell the world how you wish to dispose of your property after you die. The document is usually kept private until after your death. Then a court proceeding ("probate") tests the validity of the will. Your property will then be distributed to your heirs.

Although each state has different laws about wills, all have certain rules in common. A will usually appoints an "executor," who oversees the distribution of your property. A will directs the executor to give your property to certain persons or groups (your heirs). A will often begins by naming specific gifts of cash or property, with the balance of what you own going to a designated person or entity. You execute (sign) the will and have it signed by two or three different witnesses, the number of whom depends on the state in which you live. The witnesses need not read the will, but they must know that the document you have signed was your will. To avoid any possible problems, your will should be prepared by an attorney.

Simple wills usually are inexpensive. Some states even have sample forms that allow you to prepare your own.

For example, California has a "statutory will form" that allows you to make specific gifts of your personal residence, automobiles, household items, personal items, cash, and the balance of your property. It has boxes to fill in for your choice of guardians for your children, your choices for executor, and other matters. A copy of the California Statutory Will Form is provided in this book as Appendix B.[1]

Sometimes married people like to have what are known as "mutual wills." Mutual wills can be revoked at any time, just as with any other will.

You should always include the names of your spouse and all of your children in your will. If you omit one, that person can later claim that you simply forgot about them when you were making the will, and can claim a share of your property even if you did not intend them to have one. Such omitted children are known as "pretermitted heirs."

T rusts

You create a "trust" to receive your property and hold it for someone else. You are the "trustor." All trusts have four things in common:

- the *intent* of someone to give property to be held for the use of another person (the "beneficiary");
- *property* that is held for the use of someone else;
- the *purpose* of holding property for another; for example, you could give property to a trust now, with the purpose of distributing it to your children after you die; and
- at least one *beneficiary*.[2]

The person or group holding your trust property is known as the *trustee*. A trustee can be an individual or a corporation and needs only the legal capacity to take and hold the trust property. Trustees are required to use the utmost loyalty to control and preserve the property of the trust and to meet its objectives.

The three most common types of trusts used for estate planning purposes are trusts created by wills, revocable trusts created during someone's life, and irrevocable trusts created during the person's life. Trusts created by wills are "testamentary trusts." For example, if you think that you may die before your children are old enough to manage your property, your will can put your property in trust until your children reach some later age to be stated by you. Note that a testamentary trust will not avoid any taxes or probate fees.

To avoid probate fees (and sometimes taxes), people commonly use living *(inter vivos)* trusts. Living trusts can be either "revocable" or "irrevocable." Irrevocable trusts often have significant tax advantages. For example, if you give property to a trust to be held for your children, the income from the property is usually taxed to the trust or to your children, which presumably means at a lower tax rate than your own. However, because of exceptions to this rule, you should always check with a lawyer before forming anything as complicated as a trust.

A "revocable" trust has the advantage that you can cancel it
and take back your property. You also can manage the trust during your lifetime if you wish. A revocable living trust can also save
money; property you have given to the trust does not go through
probate proceedings and you save at least some lawyers and
executors fees. Although revocable living trusts have fewer tax
advantages than irrevocable trusts, they are the most common
estate planning devices.

Even revocable living trusts should be used with care. They are
far more expensive to draft and implement than wills. To implement a living trust, you usually need a lawyer to supervise the
transfer of title of your property to the trust. This can involve
recording real property deeds, assigning stock, changing bank
accounts, and other formalities. You also must maintain separate
bank accounts for the trust and keep careful records. There are
sometimes unfavorable income tax results associated with living
trusts, so you should first talk to a lawyer experienced in this area.

A living trust usually should be drafted at the same time as a
will, which allows the will to "pour over" property into the trust
after you have died. The will and the living trust should work
together.

One reason a person uses a living trust is that he or she can be
its trustee. In other words, you can give property to a trust for your
children and continue to manage it while you are alive. Of course,
you can select other people or a bank to act as trustees.

Wills and trusts are the two most common planning devices for
the disposition of property after death. However, many people also
plan for the management of their property if they are alive but
unable to manage the property themselves. Courts can appoint
conservators to care for your property if you become incapacitated. The simpler approach, however, is to create a Durable Power
of Attorney.

D urable Power of Attorney

A "power of attorney" is a written document that appoints another person to act in place of the person who signs the document.
An ordinary power of attorney becomes invalid if the person who
signs it later becomes unable to care for his or her own welfare.

However, a Durable Power of Attorney is effective after the person who signs the document becomes incapacitated. This allows you to appoint another person to take care of your legal, financial, and health care matters if you become unable to do so yourself.

In California, a Durable Power of Attorney is defined as "a power of attorney by which a principal designates another his or her attorney in fact in writing and the writing contains the words 'this power of attorney shall not be affected by the subsequent incapacity of the principal' or 'this power of attorney shall become effective upon the incapacitation of the principal' or similar words. . . ."[3]

There are two types of Durable Power of Attorney. A Durable Power of Attorney for Property allows someone to care for your property, but not your health. In contrast, a Durable Power of Attorney for Health Care allows your substitute to make decisions about your health care. Both documents give another person the power to make decisions for you if you lose the mental capacity to make them for yourself.

The Durable Power of Attorney for Property (DPAP) serves the same purpose as a court order appointing a "conservator" for a person who is unable to manage his or her own affairs. Generally, the DPAP is preferred since it can be created *before* you become incapacitated, you can choose the person who is appointed, and it is far less expensive and faster than a court proceeding. Conservatorships are usually recommended when you have already become incapacitated or if you suspect that your decision will later be challenged in court by family members or others. The DPAP is also similar to a living trust since the trustee would similarly be appointed to handle your property. However, the DPAP terminates when you die and does not require that property be transferred into the name of the trust. The property passes under your will.

A DPAP can be set up as you wish. It can, for instance, cover only a temporary and specific period, such as a hospital operation and recuperation, and expire when you are well. A thorough estate planning attorney often creates both a DPAP and a living trust to handle different problems that might arise.

A Durable Power of Attorney for Health Care (DPAHC) addresses your health care needs in case you become incapacitated and allows another person to make health care decisions for you if you are mentally unable to make them for yourself.

Different states have different requirements for durable powers of attorney. For example, in California the DPAHC must specifically authorize the appointed person to make health care decisions, it must contain the date of its execution, and it must be witnessed or notarized. Some states even have forms for people to use if they want a DPAHC. Appendix A is a copy of the California form for a Durable Power of Attorney for Health Care.[4]

S ummary

Everyone should make plans for the distribution of his or her property after death. At a minimum, you should have a valid will stating how you want your property distributed. It should appoint someone to govern the distribution of the property, and it should be witnessed.

If you own a good deal of property, you should also consider forming a living trust. This involves giving property to a legal entity known as a "trust," to be distributed to the people you choose after you die. Living trusts can sometimes save taxes and lawyers fees.

You should also consider creating a Durable Power of Attorney that will allow another person to manage your affairs if you become unable to manage them yourself. You can appoint someone to manage your property or make your health care decisions.

Each state has different laws about these crucial decisions, so you should check with a lawyer before you take any action. In any case, you should consider the advantages of organizing your affairs before a catastrophe occurs. Wills, trusts, and durable powers of attorney can avoid added confusion and grief for your family members if something happens to you.

R eferences

1. The California Statutory Will Form is contained in Probate Code Section 6240.
2. California Probate Code Sections 15202–205 itemize the elements necessary to create a trust. These elements might vary from state to state. California law allows the creation of trusts without specifically naming any trustee; the court can later name the trustee.
3. California Civil Code Section 2400.

4. California Civil Code Section 2432. California Civil Code Section 2433 contains a form people can use in creating a Durable Power of Attorney for Health Care.

eight

What If I Have Problems Paying My Debts?

"There is abundant evidence of the use of abusive, deceptive, and unfair debt collection practices by many debt collectors. Abusive debt collection practices contribute to the number of personal bankruptcies, to marital instability, to the loss of jobs, and to invasions of individual privacy."
—*15 U.S.C.A. Section 1692(a).*

Many people have problems paying their debts. People with disabilities are especially prone to such problems because they often have lower incomes than many other people.

Disabling accidents or chronic illness can often mean financial difficulties as well as health problems. Enormous hospital and medical costs are often associated with medical disasters and may result in bills that cannot be paid.

The best approach for people facing debt problems is to organize their affairs using a budget. You should calculate your monthly income and write it down on the left side of a piece of paper. Then add up all your monthly expenses in a column on the right side. Calculate a reserve for any once-a-year bills and for savings if possible. Remember to leave room for entertainment and transportation, as well as for clothing, food, and rent. Then live within your means; try not to violate the budget in any given month.

When financial problems occur, you may want to know about your legal rights and your duties with respect to the people to whom you owe money (your "creditors"). Creditors can garnish wages, levy bank accounts, record liens against real estate, and foreclose on secured property. To prevent these steps, you have the right to declare bankruptcy, which allows you to start with a "clean slate." Hopefully, you will not have the same monetary difficulties after filing bankruptcy.

If collection agencies dun you with impolite and obnoxious phone calls demanding payment of past due bills, you have other rights. The Fair Debt Collection Practices Act requires that debt collectors tell the truth, not swear, not talk with your employer unnecessarily, and refrain from certain other conduct. It is illegal for a collection agency to violate these rules.

If your credit rating is damaged by incorrect reports of late payments or outstanding bills, you have other rights. The Fair Credit Reporting Act requires accuracy in reporting debts to credit reporting agencies and provides procedures for contesting unfavorable reports and for correcting mistakes.

Of course, the best approach is to try to avoid problems by budgeting your income wisely and staying within your budget.

T he Powers of Creditors

A creditor is a person or entity entitled to collect money from a "debtor." If the debtor is unable to pay his or her bills, the creditor is usually required to sue in court to collect the money owed.

Sometimes creditors can repossess cars or foreclose mortgages, but in most cases the creditor is required to sue in court. Creditors can foreclose only on secured loans. If you signed an agreement giving your car or house as security for a loan, the loan is "secured." If not, it is "unsecured." If the debt is unsecured, the creditor must file a lawsuit. A copy of the lawsuit must be served upon the debtor. This means that the debtor is usually aware of all proceedings, since the United States Constitution requires that lawsuits be served in a manner that is reasonably calculated to give actual notice to the debtor. Although creditors are sometimes allowed to serve lawsuits through notices in a newspaper, they are usually required to first attempt to serve the debtor personally.

If you have been served with a lawsuit, you are entitled to file documents in court and contest the debt. Contested cases are eventually assigned to trial, where the claims are presented to a judge or jury. Both parties can appear at trial with or without lawyers in contested cases.

People served with a lawsuit must act quickly if they wish to contest it. The documents served always state the time period available for filing documents to contest the lawsuit. The time periods vary from state to state and sometimes change depending on the type of case. For example, people served with ordinary collection lawsuits in Florida have only twenty days to respond, whereas those served with similar suits in California have thirty days. You should, therefore, immediately consult an attorney if you are served with a lawsuit so that you can determine what time limits apply and what documents must be filed to protect your rights.

If you do not respond to the lawsuit in time, the case can be decided against you without the judge even considering that you might not owe the debt. This is called "judgment by default," and is just as powerful as a judgment issued after a full trial.

When creditors file lawsuits, they seek "judgments." A judgment states that the case has been decided in favor of either the creditor or the debtor. If it is in favor of the creditor, it usually states a monetary amount that the creditor is entitled to collect from the debtor.

After the creditor obtains a judgment, he or she is entitled to use the powers of the court to collect the amount stated. Creditors often are allowed to add their costs, interest, and legal fees to the amount stated in the judgment, but they are not allowed to take the law into their own hands. Even after judgment, creditors are required to use legal processes to collect what is owed them.

The legal processes that judgment creditors are entitled to use include:

- *Wage garnishment.* The process of deducting a portion of your wages each pay period until the creditor is paid in full.
- *Bank levies.* The process of seizing money you have at a bank, credit union, or savings and loan to satisfy the judgment.
- *Levy on real estate.* The process of recording a lien against any real estate you own. It can include eventually selling the real estate to pay the debt.
- *Seizure of personal property.* The process of having a sheriff or marshal seize any personal belongings you may own so that they can be sold to satisfy the debt in the lawsuit.
- *Till-tapping.* The process of installing a sheriff or marshal in any business you own to collect the money received by the business to pay the judgment.

These legal processes are available to all creditors who have obtained judgments. The actual procedures are usually performed by a sheriff or marshal, although they can sometimes be performed by licensed process servers or other people.

In most states, the two most common procedures are wage garnishment and recording of a lien against real estate. Bank levies are usually easy to perform, but creditors seldom know where to find your bank accounts. The other procedures are not as common, since forcing the sale of your house or personal property is usually time-consuming.

Regardless of which legal process creditors use to collect a debt, they must realize that debtors also have rights. Debtors are entitled to file for protection under the federal bankruptcy laws, to be free from abusive and deceptive debt collection practices, and to have credit information accurately reported. The most powerful right debtors can use is the right to file bankruptcy.

T he Right To File Bankruptcy

In medieval countries, people who did not pay their bills were sent to prison. This does not occur in the United States today, and "debtors prisons" no longer exist.

People who cannot pay their obligations are entitled to file for protection under the bankruptcy laws of the United States. Filing for bankruptcy provides people with a fresh economic start in life by legally "wiping out" most debts, and it prevents creditors from taking any action to collect debts until the bankruptcy court decides what each individual creditor can acquire from the bankrupt debtor.

Filing for bankruptcy has both pros and cons. On the one hand, people who are unable to pay their bills are legally relieved of their debt burdens and are generally permitted to retain most of their possessions. However, a bankruptcy filing usually prevents them from obtaining new credit, and social stigma is often attached to the person who has been bankrupt. In general, people who are unable to pay their bills and are constantly hounded by creditors should file for bankruptcy. Such people are usually already unable to obtain credit and sometimes already have the social stigma of being a "deadbeat."

The bankruptcy laws of the United States are contained in the current Bankruptcy Code, which was enacted as part of the Bankruptcy Reform Act of 1978.[1]

The Bankruptcy Code contains eight chapters: Chapters 1, 3, 5, 7, 9, 11, 12 and 13. (Perhaps one of the reasons that bankruptcy law seems so complicated is that the chapters are not even numbered in order!) Chapters 7, 9, 11, 12 and 13 contain specific provisions about different types of bankruptcy. Chapter 7 is the most commonly used bankruptcy procedure, allowing for a relatively quick liquidation. Chapter 9 involves bankruptcy for municipalities, such as cities. Chapter 11 is for businesses and people with large debts. Chapter 12 allows the reorganization of family farms, and Chapter 13 adjusts debts for people earning wages.

The two most common chapters used by individuals filing for bankruptcy are Chapters 7 and 13. Chapter 7 is known as a "straight" bankruptcy or a "liquidation." Individual debtors usually receive "discharges" of all debts incurred prior to filing the bankruptcy. This means they are legally relieved of all financial obligations. People usually prefer to file under Chapter 7 because of its simplicity and the chance to stop thinking about old debts and start anew.

However, some people prefer to file a Chapter 13 bankruptcy. Chapter 13 has some benefits, since a Chapter 13 filing is usually not quite as destructive to obtaining future credit as a Chapter 7 filing. Chapter 13 is available only to debtors who have unsecured debts of less than $100,000 and secured debts of less than $350,000. Chapter 13 is known as the "wage-earner plan." It is intended for people who want to pay most of their debts by rescheduling and reorganizing their financial affairs.[2]

Both Chapter 7 and Chapter 13 allow debtors to obtain discharges of debts. Both chapters also allow debtors to retain "exempt" property even after bankruptcy. Determining what property is exempt depends in part on the state in which you live. Different states have different exemptions, and some federal bankruptcy laws exempt property in all states. Property that is usually exempt includes:

- Some or all of the value of a home that you own.
- Social security payments.
- Retirement and disability payments.
- Most household goods and wearing apparel.
- A certain amount of jewelry.

Filing for bankruptcy obviously can be very complicated. You should contact a lawyer and discuss the matter thoroughly before you file a petition under any bankruptcy chapter. But remember that if you are unable to pay your debts and your liabilities exceed your assets, federal bankruptcy protection is probably available to you.

If you do not want to file bankruptcy or cannot do so, you still have the right to prevent creditors from harassing you and to prevent them from making inaccurate reports to credit reporting agencies.

P reventing Unfair Debt Collection Practices

Congress passed the Fair Debt Collection Practices Act in 1977 to prevent collection agencies from using unfair or abusive tactics to collect debts. This law affects only debt collectors, defined as people in any business "the principal purpose of which is the collection of any debts. . . ." The law does not affect the actual creditors. This means that if one of your bills is assigned to a debt collector, you are entitled to the protection of the Fair Debt Collection Practices Act. It does not apply if your bill is not assigned to a debt collector.[3]

The Fair Debt Collection Practices Act is a federal law. The Federal Trade Commission handles complaints under the federal act. Approximately half of the individual states have their own agencies to handle complaints from consumers. If you have a complaint about a debt collector, you should check first with the Federal Trade Commission to determine whether it will handle your complaint or a state agency will handle it. For example, in 1992 California eliminated its regulatory agency, which handled consumer complaints about debt collections.

The Fair Debt Collection Practices Act prevents debt collectors from using abusive, deceptive, and unfair collection practices. Specific acts that are forbidden include:

- Calling you at unusual times or places. The law assumes that it is inconvenient for debtors to be called before 8:00 in the morning or after 9:00 at night.
- Contacting you if the debt collector knows that you are represented by an attorney. Of course, if your attorney fails to respond within a reasonable period, the debt collector is allowed to contact you.
- Calling other people. Debt collectors cannot call other people, such as your employer, unless it is necessary to locate you or to collect a judgment, or with your permission.
- Contacting you after you have notified the collector that you do not want more calls. If you have notified a debt collector in writing that you wish him or her to cease further communication with you, the debt collector cannot communicate with you further except to notify you of legal remedies or that collection efforts are being terminated.
- Threatening the use of violence. Debt collectors cannot harass you by threatening violence.
- Using obscene or profane language. Debt collectors cannot swear at you.
- Causing your telephone to ring repeatedly to annoy you.
- Using false, deceptive, or misleading representations. Debt collectors cannot lie to you or send you false legal documents.

The Fair Debt Collection Practices Act also requires that debt collectors promptly notify you of the amount of the debt and the name of the creditor to whom the debt is owed. If you dispute a debt, you should notify the collector within thirty days after receipt of the notice that specifies the amount owed. The collector is then required to obtain verification of the debt and send a copy to you.

If debt collectors violate these rules, they are liable to you for monetary damages. You are entitled to collect from them (1) any actual damage you sustained; (2) punitive damages of up to $1,000; and (3) your attorneys fees and court costs. Of course, when the law allows you to recover your "attorneys fees" it means that you can only recover them if you take the case all the way to trial. Even then, the judge often decreases the amount awarded to you to a rate far below what attorneys normally charge.

If a debt collector has violated these laws, you should first check with the Federal Trade Commission and then with any state agencies. Contact a lawyer if you still cannot obtain satisfaction.

Collection agencies and other creditors are also required to make accurate reports to credit reporting agencies. Although many credit reports contain inaccurate information, people have the right to accuracy in credit reporting.

T he Right to Accurate Credit Reporting

Congress passed the Fair Credit Reporting Act (FCRA) in 1970 to ensure that consumer reporting agencies are fair, impartial, and respect people's rights to privacy. The FCRA requires consumer reporting agencies to adopt reasonable procedures that are fair and equitable to consumers. The act affects only "consumer reports," which are reports about a person's credit standing, character, reputation, or mode of living and which are used for credit, insurance, or employment purposes.

The Fair Credit Reporting Act limits the circumstances under which a consumer reporting agency can furnish a consumer report. Credit reports can only be furnished (1) in response to a court order; (2) in response to written instructions from the consumer; and (3) to a person who intends to use the information in connection with a credit transaction involving the consumer or for employment, insurance, or licensing purposes, or for an otherwise legitimate need in connection with a business transaction involving the consumer.

Consumer reporting agencies must delete all obsolete information. Specifically, they must delete the following:

- Reports about bankruptcies that are more than ten years old.
- Old judgments. Consumer reporting agencies must delete information regarding judgments more than seven years old or after expiration of the governing statute of limitations.
- Tax liens paid more than seven years ago.
- Accounts placed for collection or written off more than seven years ago.
- Arrest or conviction records that are more than seven years old.
- Any other adverse information that is more than seven years old.

These rules involve only transactions with principle amounts of less than $50,000. Obsolete information can be reported in connection with credit transactions or insurance of $50,000 or more, and employment with annual salaries of $20,000 or more.

One of the main purposes of the FCRA is to ensure accurate credit reporting. Some studies have shown that many credit reports contain inaccurate information. However, the FCRA requires that consumer reporting agencies "follow reasonable procedures to assure maximum possible accuracy of the information concerning the individual about whom the report relates."[4]

The FCRA tries to ensure accuracy in credit reporting by giving consumers the right to challenge inaccurate reports. If you wish to correct your credit report, you should first start by obtaining a copy of it.

Section 1681g of the Act requires that all reporting agencies provide you with a copy of your credit report upon request. You must give reasonable notice of your desire to see your credit report and must furnish proper identification to the reporting agency.

After you have obtained a copy of your credit report, you are entitled to dispute the completeness or accuracy of any item of information. You should write a letter to the credit reporting agency stating that you dispute the items. The letter should contain a brief statement explaining the dispute. The law allows reporting agencies to limit such statements to not more than one hundred words.

If you notify a consumer reporting agency that you dispute any information on a credit report, the agency is usually required to reinvestigate the information by contacting the creditor who reported it. If the reinvestigation shows that the information is inaccurate, or if the information cannot be verified, the reporting agency is required to delete it. Even if the creditor confirms that the information is correct, the reporting agency is required to note that you filed a statement of dispute unless the dispute is resolved.[5]

If you are denied credit insurance or employment because of a consumer report, the company that received the report must notify you and supply the name and address of the consumer reporting agency that made the report. Often this is how people learn of inaccurate information on their credit reports. If you receive such a notification, you are entitled to obtain a free copy of your credit report from the agency that supplied the report, within thirty days. Then you can follow the procedures outlined previously to dispute any inaccurate information.

If a consumer reporting agency or a user of information willfully breaks this law, it is liable to you for (1) actual damages sustained by you; (2) punitive damages if allowed by a court; and (3) your reasonable costs and attorneys fees. If the credit reporting agency or user of information acted negligently (not intentionally), the consumer cannot obtain punitive damages. Again, remember that courts usually decrease the amount of attorneys fees awarded in such cases to amounts far below what attorneys normally charge. This means that you should contact an attorney if you believe that your rights under the Fair Credit Reporting Act have been violated. Discuss the costs of proceeding, and weigh those costs against the possible benefits of suing to enforce your rights.

R eferences

1. The Bankruptcy Reform Act of 1978 enacted a new Title 11 to the United States Code.
2. 11 U.S.C. § 109(e). The limitation of the maximum amount of debt for people filing under Chapter 13 may change. You should check with a lawyer before selecting any particular chapter of bankruptcy filing.

3. The Fair Debt Collection Practices Act is found at 15 U.S.C. § 1692 et seq.
4. 15 U.S.C. § 1681e.
5. 15 U.S.C. 1681i.

How Do I Enforce My Rights?

"Okay, now we've got the ADA; so what?"
—*Anonymous Member of Audience at MS Society's Seminar on Employment Law and the ADA.*

When the ADA was first passed, it did not contain any provisions allowing people to sue for monetary damages for violation of its rules—the new law had no "teeth." Courts could not award money to private individuals injured by a violation of the ADA. Only the Attorney General could be awarded money for violations of the ADA. This meant that it was difficult for people whose rights were violated to hire attorneys to represent them. Because people were usually not able to hire lawyers on a "contingency fee" basis, such that the attorney would receive payment only if a suit was settled in his client's favor, they were forced to pay lawyers on an hourly basis if they needed representation. Most people could not afford this. The ADA allowed courts to award attorneys fees to people who suffered discrimination, but courts often awarded far too little for the work invested in these cases.

This prompted many people to believe that the ADA did not amount to much. Although the new law received a lot of attention from the media, it did not seem that it would be enforced by private people whose rights were violated.

The Civil Rights Act of 1991 changed that. It not only allows courts to award money to compensate people for violations of the ADA but also allows courts to award *punitive* damages. If the violation of the ADA is intentional, people can be compensated with up to $50,000 for violations by companies with 100 or fewer employees, $100,000 for companies with 200 or fewer, $200,000 for companies with 500 or fewer, and $300,000 for companies with 500 or more employees. If the violation is "malicious," the offender can also be penalized with punitive damages.[1]

The new provisions in the Civil Rights Act of 1991 apply only to *employment* discrimination. Individuals still cannot be awarded monetary damages for violations of the *accessibility* laws of the ADA.

If your rights to the accessibility rules of the ADA are violated, you can only sue for "injunctive relief." This means that a court can only order the offender to provide the legally required access. Courts cannot award money to individuals for violations of the access rules; only the Department of Justice can obtain money from the offender.

If you believe that your rights have been violated, you should first make a complaint to the appropriate government agencies. You should also contact a lawyer experienced in this field.

M aking Complaints to Government Agencies

The first step in enforcing your rights under the ADA is to make a complaint to all appropriate government agencies.

First, start by contacting the federal agency that handles the type of claim for discrimination you have suffered. If you are complaining about a violation of the accessibility rules of the ADA, contact the Department of Justice:

OFFICE ON THE AMERICANS WITH DISABILITIES ACT
CIVIL RIGHTS DIVISION
U.S. DEPARTMENT OF JUSTICE
P.O. BOX 66118
WASHINGTON, DC 20035-6118
(202) 514-0301 (VOICE)
(202) 514-0381 (TDD)
(202) 514-0383 (TDD)

The Washington office of the Department of Justice can direct you to a local office and to state agencies that may also help you. If you are complaining about a violation of the ADA's employment rules, contact the Equal Employment Opportunity Commission:

EQUAL EMPLOYMENT OPPORTUNITY COMMISSION
1801 L STREET NW
WASHINGTON, DC 20507
(202) 663-4900 (VOICE)
800-800-3302 (TDD)
(202) 663-4494 (TDD - FOR 202 AREA CODE)

The Washington office of the EEOC can also direct you to a local office, or possibly to a state agency handling similar claims. The EEOC and the Department of Justice are the main federal agencies that handle ADA complaints. However, some other departments can provide you with information.

If you need specific information about the ADA's rules regarding transportation, contact:

DEPARTMENT OF TRANSPORTATION
400 SEVENTH STREET SW
WASHINGTON, DC 20590
(202) 366-9305 (VOICE)
(202) 755-7687 (TDD)

If you are interested in obtaining specific information about the design requirements and architectural standards of the ADA, contact:

ARCHITECTURAL AND TRANSPORTATION BARRIERS COMPLIANCE BOARD
1111 18TH STREET NW
SUITE 501
WASHINGTON, DC 20036
800-USA-ABLE (VOICE)
800-USA-ABLE (TDD)

The telecommunications rules of the ADA can be explained by the Federal Communications Commission:

FEDERAL COMMUNICATIONS COMMISSION
1919 M STREET NW
WASHINGTON, DC 20554
(202) 632-7260 (VOICE)
(202) 632-6999 (TDD)

When you are making a complaint to a government agency, consider the following suggestions:

1. Act quickly. There are critical deadlines that you must meet. If you are not timely, you can lose your right to bring suit against the offender. For example, you must file an employment discrimination claim within 180 days of the violation.
2. Focus your complaint. Many people file complaints in anger and mention everything but violations of the law. When you file a complaint, you should focus on violations of the law and how such violations were harmful to you. This will allow the government investigators to clearly see the important facts of your case.
3. Provide evidence. Agencies such as the EEOC receive hundreds of complaints from disgruntled former employees. The complaints are often unfounded. If you have photographic or documentary proof of your complaint, provide it to the agency.
4. Give names and dates. Give as much information to the agency as possible, so that they know who to contact, who

to interview, and when specific events occurred.

5. If you are complaining about employment discrimination, you must process your claim with the EEOC before you file a lawsuit. The EEOC will review your complaint. It can issue an "accusation" (an administrative procedure) against the offender, or can even file a court suit on your behalf. If the EEOC does not take action for you, it will send you a letter allowing you to file your own court suit. This is known as a "Notice of Right To Sue." After you have received this letter, you can sue the offender in court.

6. If your complaint is about a violation of your rights to public access (a violation of Title II or III of the ADA), you can file a complaint with the Department of Justice. Like the EEOC, the DOJ can file a court suit for you. However, you can file your own court suit without first complaining to the DOJ.

Often you must go to the agency office in person to sign the complaint. There usually is an office located near your town or city. You can call the agencies listed previously to find the location of the office nearest you.

H iring a Lawyer

It is usually advisable to hire a lawyer as soon as possible to supervise the submission of your complaint to the government agency. However, it is imperative that you find a lawyer experienced in handling similar cases. If you know a lawyer personally, you can ask him or her for a referral to someone who is experienced in disability rights law issues. Otherwise you can obtain a referral from your local county bar association or a local disability organization. A phone call to your local branch of the United Cerebral Palsy Association, Multiple Sclerosis Society, or similar organization may help.

After you find a lawyer experienced in handling this type of case, you should meet with him or her to see if you feel comfortable. Try to find a lawyer you think is honest, trustworthy, and willing to work for your best interests. Remember that a lawyer must be a "counselor." Your lawyer must be able to give you advice, and you must have confidence in his or her ability.

If you need to hire a lawyer, you should consider the following suggestions:

1. Look for someone who is experienced in the legal aspect of your case. Like all other things in American society, law has become very complicated. Most lawyers are specialized; while lawyers in some rural areas can maintain general practices, lawyers in most urban areas focus on one or more fields of law. Try to find someone experienced in the particular field involving your case.
2. Do not be bashful. Discuss your lawyer's experience in this particular field with him or her. Ask about prior cases handled and if he or she specializes in this particular field of law.
3. Do not be afraid to discuss payment arrangements with your prospective attorney. You are contemplating a financial relationship, and both you and your attorney must see eye-to-eye about the payment arrangement. This means it is usually best to discuss these matters in person.
4. Remember that your lawyer is human. People sometimes search for a superhuman lawyer who can win any case, even a bad one. Only Perry Mason won every case; in real life lawyers tend to win good cases and lose bad ones. If you have a bad case, encourage your lawyer to tell you this so that you can avoid the time, aggravation, and expense of a losing lawsuit.
5. Beware of promises. Lawyers cannot promise anything. Their results are almost always dependent on what a judge or jury determines. Obviously, since your lawyer is neither the judge nor a member of the jury, he or she cannot guarantee the result. Any lawyer who attempts to guarantee a result should be viewed with caution.

If you are going to hire a lawyer, you should always have a written retainer agreement that clearly sets forth the scope of the work, the basis of the charges, the hourly rate to be charged (if any), and anything else you think is important.

Sometimes lawyers are willing to take cases on what is called a "contingency fee" basis. This means that the lawyer does not receive any fee other than a percentage of the amount that may be awarded to you. Keep in mind that lawyers are only likely to take your case on a contingency fee basis if you have a very good case. Like everyone else, lawyers need to make money; if they do not expect you to win the case, you cannot expect them to work for a percentage of your possible winnings!

If your lawyer does agree to take your case on a contingency fee basis, you should get a written agreement that specifies the percentage that you have agreed upon and states how the advances for costs will affect your recovery. "Court costs" can be substantial. Filing fees, deposition transcripts, expert witness fees, and other costs can often quickly add up to thousands of dollars. Your written agreement should spell out your arrangement regarding these costs. As with anything else, the advice to "get it in writing" also applies to hiring your attorney.

O nly a Lawyer Can Give Legal Advice

If you have any specific questions about your particular case, you should consult a lawyer as soon as possible. Although this book attempts to explain various areas of the law, it obviously cannot address every situation for every person. Each case is unique, and yours may involve a legal issue that is slightly different from any of the issues discussed in this book.

Moreover, American laws constantly change. The changing process that created the ADA and the body of law known as "disability rights law" is also changing all of the laws discussed in this book. Some of them may have changed between the time this was written and the time it went to press. The legal documents in the appendices may even have changed.

Justice Oliver Wendell Holmes once said, "The development of our law has gone on for nearly a thousand years, like the development of a plant, each generation taking the inevitable next step, mind like matter, simply obeying a law of spontaneous growth." *Because of the constant and spontaneous changes in the law, you need a lawyer to deal with your particular issue, even if it is clearly described in this book.*[2]

This book is intended to be a guide and to explain general rules about the law. It is not intended to deal with any particular situation or case. Its intent is simply to describe the developing "plant" mentioned by Justice Holmes.

References

1. Public Law 102-166, Section 102.
2. Holmes, *The Path of the Law,* 10 Harv. L. Rev., 61 (1897).

A ppendix A

C alifornia's Statutory Form for a Durable Power of Attorney for Health Care

California law provides a form for a Durable Power of Attorney for Health Care. Please note that this law is only valid in California, and only affects residents of that state. While the form might be effective in other states, it is purely a creation of the California legislature.

The California form must contain the following statement:

WARNING TO PERSON EXECUTING THIS DOCUMENT

This is an important legal document. Before executing this document, you should know these important facts:

This document gives the person you designate as your agent (the attorney in fact) the power to make health care decisions for you. Your agent must act consistently with your desires as stated in this document or otherwise made known.

Except as you otherwise specify in this document, this document gives your agent the power to consent to your doctor not giving treatment or stopping treatment necessary to keep you alive.

Notwithstanding this document, you have the right to make medical and other health care decisions for yourself so long as you can give informed consent with respect to the particular decision. In addition, no treatment may be given to you over your objection, and health care necessary to keep you alive may not be stopped or withheld if you object at the time.

This document gives your agent authority to consent, to refuse to consent, or to withdraw consent to any care, treatment, service, or procedure to maintain, diagnose, or treat a physical or mental condition. This power is subject to any statement of your desires and any limitations that you include in this document. You may state in this document any types of treatment that you do not desire. In addition, a court can take away the power of your agent to make health care decisions for you if your agent (1) authorized anything that is illegal, (2) acts contrary to your known desires, or (3) where your desires are not known, does anything that is clearly contrary to your best interests.

This power will exist for an indefinite period of time unless you limit its duration in this document.

You have the right to revoke the authority of your agent by notifying your agent or your treating doctor, hospital, or other health care provider orally or in writing of the revocation.

Your agent has the right to examine your medical records and to consent to their disclosure unless you limit this right in this document.

Unless you otherwise specify in this document, this document gives your agent the power after you die to (1) authorize an autopsy, (2) donate your body or parts thereof for transplant or therapeutic or educational or scientific purposes, and (3) direct the disposition of your remains.

If there is anything in this document that you do not understand, you should ask a lawyer to explain it to you.

(California law requires that a durable power of attorney specifically authorize the attorney in fact to make health care decisions. Therefore, you should include language similar to the following):

With full knowledge of the above, and being of sound mind and body, I specifically authorize _____ [fill in name of person you wish to make health care decisions] to make health care decisions for me and on my behalf. This includes but is not limited to the authority to consent, to refuse to consent or to withdraw consent to any care, treatment, service or procedure to maintain, diagnose or treat a physical or mental condition. It also includes the power to consent to my doctor not giving treatment or stopping treatment necessary to keep me alive. It also includes the power after I die to authorize an autopsy, donate my body or parts thereof for transplant or therapeutic or educational or scientific purposes, and direct the disposition of my remains.

Dated: _____ [Fill in date of execution]

_____ [Sign here]

(This form must either be witnessed or notarized. If the form is witnessed, each witness must sign the following statement):

I declare under penalty of perjury under the laws of California that the person who signed or acknowledged this document is personally known to me to be the principal, or that the identity of the principal was proved to me by convincing evidence, that the principal signed or acknowledged this Durable Power of Attorney in my presence, that the principal appears to be of sound mind and under no duress, fraud or undue influence, that I am not the person appointed as attorney in fact by this document, and that I am not the principal's health care provider, an employee of the principal's health care provider, the operator of a community care facility, an employee of an operator of a community care facility, the operator of a residential care facility for the elderly, nor an employee of an operator of a residential care facility for the elderly.

(At least one of the witnesses must also sign the following declaration):

I further declare under penalty of perjury under the laws of California that I am not related to the principal by blood, marriage, or adoption, and to the best of my knowledge, I am not entitled to any part of the estate of the principal upon the death of the principal under a will now existing or by operation of law.

Dated: _____ [Fill in date of execution]

_____ [Witness signs here]

[Please note that the witnesses cannot be any of the people excluded by the wording of the witness signature form provided above. Also note that the attorney in fact cannot be the treating health care provider, nor an operator of a community care facility or residential care facility for the elderly, nor an employee of any of those entities. Also note that the attorney in fact cannot be the principal's conservator except under certain specific conditions.

The Durable Power of Attorney for Health Care is not effective if the person executing it is not mentally competent, or if the person executing it is in a nursing home (except under certain specific circumstances). If the form used above is handwritten, it must be in capital letters. It must also contain the following certificate from a lawyer]:

I am a lawyer authorized to practice law in the state where this power of attorney was executed, and the principal was my client at the time this power of attorney was executed. I have advised my client concerning his or her rights in connection with this power of attorney and the applicable law and the consequences of signing or not signing this power of attorney, and my client, after being so advised, has executed this power of attorney.

Dated: _____ [Fill in date of execution]

_____ [Signature of Attorney]

As with all other matters, if you have any specific questions about this, you should consult an attorney. This form may not be sufficient to meet the specific demands of your unique situation. It is provided simply to show readers what is usually included in a Durable Power of Attorney for Health Care.

This form was current as of the beginning of 1993, but note that laws change and the laws that created this form may have changed, too. For changes, see California Civil Code Section 2433.

A ppendix B

C alifornia Statutory Will Form

California law provides a form you can use for a will. Please note that this form is valid only in the state of California. It is contained in California Probate Code Section 6240. This Probate Code Section was up-to-date at the beginning of 1993, but may have been changed since then.

In any event, it is suggested that you consult an attorney to prepare your will. Mistakes in wills can result in their being found invalid by a court. This means that even the slightest mistake can often result in catastrophic consequences. This will is provided as a convenience, not to be used in each unique situation.

• • •

The following is the California statutory will form:

QUESTIONS AND ANSWERS
ABOUT THIS CALIFORNIA STATUTORY WILL

The following information, in question and answer form, is not a part of the California Statutory Will. It is designed to help you understand about Wills and to decide if this Will meets your needs. This Will is in a simple form. The complete text of each paragraph of this Will is printed at the end of the Will.

1. *What happens if I die without a Will?* If you die without a Will, what you own (your "assets") in your name alone will be divided among your spouse, children, or other relatives according to state law. The court will appoint a relative to collect and distribute your assets.

2. *What can a Will do for me?* In a Will you may designate who will receive your assets at your death. You may designate someone (called an "executor") to appear before the court, collect your assets, pay your debts and taxes, and distribute your assets as you specify. You may nominate someone (called a "guardian") to raise your children who are under age 18. You may designate someone (called a "custodian") to manage assets for your children until they reach any age between 18 and 25.

3. *Does a Will avoid probate?* No. With or without a Will, assets in your name along usually go through the court probate process. The court's first job is to determine if your Will is valid.

4. *What is community property?* Can I give away my share in my Will? If you are married and you or your spouse earned money during your marriage from work and wages, that money (and the assets bought with it) is community property. Your Will can only give away your one-half of community property. Your Will cannot give away your spouse's one-half of community property.

5. *Does my Will give away all of my assets?* Do all assets go through probate? No. Money in a joint tenancy bank account automatically belongs to the other named owner without probate. If your spouse or child is on the deed to your house as a joint tenant, the house automatically passes to him or her. Life insurance and retirement plan benefits may pass directly to the named beneficiary. A Will does not necessarily control how these types of "nonprobate" assets pass at your death.

6. *Are there different kinds of Wills?* Yes. There are handwritten Wills, typewritten Wills, attorney-prepared Wills, and statutory Wills. All are valid if done precisely as the law requires. You should see a lawyer if you do not want to use this statutory Will or if you do not understand this form.

7. *Who may use this Will?* This Will is based on California law. It is designed only for California residents. You may use this form if you are single, married, or divorced. You must be age 18 or older and of sound mind.

8. *Are there any reasons why I should NOT use this statutory Will?* Yes. This is a simple Will. It is not designed to reduce

death taxes or other taxes. Talk to a lawyer to do tax planning, especially if (i) your assets will be worth more than
$600,000 at your death, (ii) you own business related assets,
(iii) you want to create a trust fund for your children's education or other purposes, (iv) you own assets in some other
state, (v) you want to disinherit your spouse or descendants,
or (vi) you have valuable interests in pension or profit shar-
ing plans. You should talk to a lawyer who knows about
estate planning if this Will does not meet your needs. This
Will treats most adopted children like natural children. You
should talk to a lawyer if you have stepchildren or foster children whom you have not adopted.

9. *May I add or cross our any words on this Will?* No. If you do,
   the Will may be invalid or the court may ignore the crossed
   out or added words. You may only fill in the blanks. You may
   amend this Will by a separate document (called a codicil). Talk
   to a lawyer if you want to do something with your assets
   which is not allowed in this form.

10. *May I change my Will?* Yes. A Will is not effective until you die.
    You may make and sign a new Will. You may change your
    Will at any time, but only by an amendment (called a codi-
    cil). You can give away or sell your assets before your death.
    Your Will only acts on what you own at death.

11. *Where should I keep my Will?* After you and the witnesses sign
    the Will, keep your Will in your safe deposit box or other safe
    place. You should tell trusted family members where your Will
    is kept.

12. *When should I change my Will?* You should make and sign a
    new Will if you marry or divorce after you sign this Will. Divorce
    or annulment automatically cancels all property stated to pass
    to a former husband or wife under this Will and revokes the
    designation of a former spouse as executor, custodian, or
    guardian. You should sign a new Will when you have more chil-
    dren, or if your spouse or a child dies. You may want to change
    your Will if there is a large change in the value of your assets.

13. *What can I do if I do not understand something in this Will?*
    If there is anything in this Will you do not understand, ask a
    lawyer to explain it to you.

14. *What is an executor?* An "executor" is the person you name to collect your assets, pay your debts and taxes, and distribute your assets as the court directs. It may be a person or it may be a qualified bank or trust company.

15. *Should I require a bond?* You may require that an executor post a "bond." A bond is a form of insurance to replace assets that may be mismanaged or stolen by the executor. The cost of the bond is paid from the estate's assets.

16. *What is a guardian?* Do I need to designate one? If you have children under age 18, you should designate a guardian of their "persons" to raise them.

17. *What is a custodian?* Do I need to designate one? A "custodian" is a person you may designate to manage assets for someone (including a child) who is between ages 18 and 25 and who receives assets under your Will. The custodian manages the assets and pays as much as the custodian determines is proper for health, support, maintenance, and education. The custodian delivers what is left to the person when the person reaches the age you choose (between 18 and 25). No bond is required of a custodian.

18. *Should I ask people if they are willing to serve before I designate them as executor, guardian, or custodian?* Probably yes. Some people and banks and trust companies may not consent to serve or may not be qualified to act.

19. *What happens if I make a gift in this Will to someone and they die before I do?* A person must survive you by 120 hours to take a gift under a Will. If they do not, then the gift fails and goes with the rest of your assets. If the person who does not survive you is a relative of you or your spouse, then certain assets may go to the relative's descendants.

20. *What is a trust?* There are many kinds of trusts, including trusts created by Wills (called "testamentary trusts") and trusts created during your lifetime (called "revocable living trusts"). Both kinds of trusts are long-term arrangements where a manager (called a "trustee") invests and manages assets for someone (called a "benefactor") on the terms you specify. Trusts are too complicated to be used in this statutory Will. You should see a lawyer if you want to create a trust.

INSTRUCTIONS

1. READ THE WILL. Read the Will first. If you do not understand something, ask a lawyer to explain it to you.

2. FILL IN THE BLANKS. Fill in the blanks. Follow the instructions in the form carefully. Do not add any words to the Will (except for filling in blanks) or cross out any words

3. DATE AND SIGN THE WILL AND HAVE TWO WITNESSES SIGN IT. Date and sign the Will and have two witnesses sign it. You and the witnesses should read and follow the Notice to Witnesses found at the end of the Will.

CALIFORNIA STATUTORY WILL OF

> Print Your Full Name

1. <u>Will.</u> This is my Will. I revoke all prior Wills and codicils.
2. <u>Specific Gift of Personal Residence</u> (Optional—use only if you want to give your personal residence to a different person or persons than you give the balance of your assets to under paragraph 5 below). I give my interest in my principal residence at the time of my death (subject to mortgages and liens) as follows:
   (Select one choice only and sign in the box after your choice).

a. <u>Choice One:</u> All to my spouse, if my spouse survives me; otherwise to my descendants (my children and the descendants of my children) who survive me.

b. <u>Choice Two:</u> Nothing to my spouse; all to my descendants (my children and the descendants of my children) who survive me.

c. <u>Choice Three:</u> All to the following person if he or she survives me: (Insert the name of the person):

d. <u>Choice Four:</u> Equally among the following persons who survive me: (Insert the names of two or more persons):

_____
_____
_____
_____

3. <u>Specific Gift of Automobiles, Household and Personal Effects</u> (Optional - use only if you want to give automobiles and household or personal effects to a different person or persons than you give the balance of your assets to under paragraph 5 below). I give all of my automobiles (subject to loans), furniture, furnishings, household items, clothing, jewelry, and other tangible articles of a personal nature at the time of my death as follows:

(Select one choice only and sign in the box after your choice).

a. <u>Choice One:</u> All to my spouse, if my spouse survives me; otherwise to my descendants (my children and the descendants of my children) who survive me.

b. <u>Choice Two:</u> Nothing to my spouse; all to my descendants (my children and the descendants of my children) who survive me.

c. <u>Choice Three:</u> All to the following person if he or she survives me: (Insert the name of the person):

_____

d. <u>Choice Four:</u> Equally among the following persons who survive me: (Insert the names of two or more persons):

_____
_____
_____
_____

4. <u>Specific Gifts of Cash.</u> (Optional) I make the following cash gifts to the persons named below who survive me, or to the named charity, and I sign my name in the box after each gift. If I don't sign in the box, I do not make a gift. (Sign in the box after each gift you make.)

Name of Person or Charity to receive gift (name one only—please print)	Amount of Cash Gift
	Sign your name in this box to make this gift

Name of Person or Charity to receive gift (name one only—please print)	Amount of Cash Gift
	Sign your name in this box to make this gift

Name of Person or Charity to receive gift (name one only—please print)	Amount of Cash Gift
	Sign your name in this box to make this gift

Name of Person or Charity to receive gift (name one only—please print)	Amount of Cash Gift
	Sign your name in this box to make this gift

Name of Person or Charity to receive gift (name one only—please print)	Amount of Cash Gift
	Sign your name in this box to make this gift

5. <u>Balance of My Assets.</u> Except for the specific gifts made in paragraphs 2, 3, and 4 above, I give the balance of my assets as follows:
(Select <u>one</u> choice only and sign in the box after your choice. If I sign in more than one box or if I don't sign in any box, the court will distribute my assets as if I did not make a Will).

a. <u>Choice One:</u> All to my spouse, if my spouse survives me; otherwise to my descendants (my children and the descendants of my children) who survive me.

b. <u>Choice Two:</u> Nothing to my spouse; all to my descendants (my children and the descendants of my children) who survive me.

c. <u>Choice Three:</u> All to the following person if he or she survives me: (Insert the name of the person):

d. <u>Choice Four:</u> Equally among the following persons who survive me: (Insert the names of two or more persons):

6. <u>Guardian of the Child's Person.</u> If I have a child under age 18 and the child does not have a living parent at my death, I nominate the individual named below as First Choice as guardian of the person of such child (to raise the child). If the First Choice does not serve, then I nominate the Second Choice, and then the Third Choice, to serve. Only an individual (not a bank or trust company) may serve.

Name of First Choice for Guardian of the Person

Name of Second Choice for Guardian of the Person

Name of Third Choice for Guardian of the Person

7. <u>Special Provision of Property of Persons Under Age 25.</u> (Optional—Unless you use this paragraph, assets that go to a child or other person who is under age 18 may be given to the parent of the person, or to the guardian named in paragraph 6 above as guardian of the person until age 18, and the court will require a bond; and assets that go to a child or other

person who is age 18 or older will be given outright to the person. By using this paragraph you may provide that a custodian will hold the assets for the person until the person reaches any age between 18 and 25 which you choose). If a beneficiary of this Will is between age 18 and 25, I nominate the individual or bank or trust company named below as First Choice as custodian of the property. If the First Choice does not serve, then I nominate the Second Choice, and then the Third Choice, to serve.

> Name of First Choice for Custodian of Assets

> Name of Second Choice for Custodian of Assets

> Name of Third Choice for Custodian of Assets

Insert any age between 18 and 25 as the age for the person to receive the property:
(If you do not choose an age, age 18 will apply.)

8. I nominate the individual or bank or trust company named below as First Choice as executor. If the First Choice does not serve, then I nominate the Second Choice, and then the Third Choice, to serve.

> Name of First Choice for Executor

> Name of Second Choice for Executor

> Name of Third Choice for Executor

9. <u>Bond.</u> My signature in this box means a bond is *not* required for any person named as executor. A bond may be required if I do not sign in this box:

No bond shall be required

(Notice: You must sign this Will in the presence of two (2) adult witnesses. The witnesses must sign their names in your presence and in each other's presence. You must first read to them the following two sentences.)

This is my Will. I ask the persons who sign below to be my witnesses.

Signed on _____ at _____, California.
              (date)   (city)

Signature of Maker of Will

(<u>Notice to Witnesses:</u> Two (2) adults must sign as witnesses. Each witness must read the following clause before signing. The witnesses should not receive assets under this Will.)

Each of us declares under penalty of perjury under the laws of the State of California that the following is true and correct:

   a. On the date written below the maker of this Will declared to us that this instrument was the maker's Will and requested us to act as witnesses to it;

   b. We understand this is the maker's Will;

   c. The maker signed this Will in our presence, all of us being present at the same time;

   d. We now, at the maker's request, and in the maker's and each other's presence, sign below as witnesses;

   e. We believe the maker is of sound mind and memory;

   f. We believe that this Will was not procured by duress, menace, fraud or undue influence.

   g. The maker is age 18 or older; and

   h. Each of us is now age 18 or older, is a competent witness, and resides at the address set forth after his or her name.

Dated:_____,_____

Signature of witness	Signature of witness

Print name here   Print name here

_____   _____

Residence address   Residence address

_____   _____

_____   _____

AT LEAST TWO WITNESSES <u>MUST</u> SIGN
NOTARIZATION ALONE IS NOT SUFFICIENT

*I*ndex

A

Accessibility, 61–74
  changes in existing public areas
    under Title II, 64
  of a business's public areas, 63, 66
  violations of access rights, 72
Alcoholism, treatment of under
    ADA, 26
Americans With Disabilities Act
    (1990), 2, 4
  goals of, 5
  penalties for violations of, 55
Architectural and Transportation
    Barriers Compliance Board, 120
  Architectural Barriers Act
    (1968), 4

B

Bankruptcy, 109
Bankruptcy Reform Act (1978), 109
Barrier removal, 67–69
  alternatives to, 69
  examples of, 68
  in existing businesses, 67

C

Civil Rights Act (1964), 3, 9, 118
Civil Rights Act (1991), 7
Commerce Clause, as applicable to
    ADA, 6
Creditor, 106–108
  definition of, 106
  legal processes involving, 108

D

Department of Justice, 119
Department of Transportation, 119
Disability, 13–28
  ADA definition of, 14
  application of term *regarded as
    having,* 22
  categories excluded from, 24
  definition of for Social Security
    purposes, 88

definitions of under other laws, 27
Disability rights, as civil rights, 2, 3
Disability rights law, as a body of
    law, 8
Discrimination, in applying for jobs,
    48
  in compensation, 50
  establishing case of, 52
  penalties for, 55
Durable power of attorney, 102
  for health care, 102

E

Education for All Handicapped Chil-
    dren Act (1975), 4
Equal Employment Opportunity
    Commission, 119
Essential functions, as defined under
    Title I, 44

F

Fair Credit Reporting Act (1970), 112
Fair Debt Collection Practices Act
    (1977), 110
  prevention of abusive collection
    practices under, 111
Fair Housing Act (1975), 4
Federal Communications Commis-
    sion, 120
Federal preemption, 6
Fundamental job duties, under Title
    I, 42

H

Health care, access to for people
    with disabilities, 78
Health insurance, access to for peo-
    ple with disabilities, 78
  legal protection, 78
  managing problems of, 81

I

Impairment, 15–17
  as limiting major life activities, 17

definition of under ADA, 15
exclusions, 16

J

Job discrimination, 31–57
applicability to small employers, 32
treatment under Title I of the ADA,
31
Judgment, 107
by default, 107

L

Legal assistance, 122
Limiting condition, past record of, 21
Living trust, 100

M

Medicare, 86, 92–95
applying for, 95
deductible expenses under, 94
hospital insurance component of,
92
medical insurance component of,
94
Mutual will, 99

P

Power of attorney, 101
Preemployment medical test, 47
Preexisting condition, 80
Public accommodation, 62–65
definition of, 62
located in private homes, 67,
publicly owned, 70
Public transportation, under Title II,
71

Q

Qualified individual with a disability,
ADA definition of, 41

R

"Readily achievable," definition of,
65
"Reasonable accommodation," 32–36
definition of, 33, 36
examples of, 35
standard for, 40

Rehabilitation Act (1973), 7
lawsuits involving, 43
Revocable trust, 100

S

Social Security, 86–90
applying for, 89
for people with disabilities, 87
State laws, governing disability
rights, 8
as applicable to health insurance,
81
Statutory will, 99
Supplemental Security Income, 86,
90–92
applying for, 91
criteria for receiving, 91

T

Television Decoder Circuitry Act
(1990), 7
Testamentary trust, 100
Title Five, of ADA, 7
Title Four, of ADA, 7
Title One, of ADA, 5, 6
main concepts of, 45
penalties for violations of, 55
Title Three, of ADA, 7, 61
Title Two, of ADA, 6, 61
application to public transporta-
tion, 71
impact of, 70
Trust, definition of, 100

U

Undue hardship, 36–41
cost as a factor in, 38
definition of, 37
examples of, 38
Unemployment, in people with disabilities, 4
Urban Mass Transportation Act
(1970), 4

W

Will, definition of, 98, 99